The Extreme Earth

Waterfalls

Patricia Corrigan

Foreword by
Geoffrey H. Nash, Geologist

CHELSEA HOUSE
PUBLISHERS
An imprint of Infobase Publishing

*In grateful appreciation of all the workers in state and national parks, forests,
and protected scenic areas all over the world who make it possible
for the rest of us to understand and treasure the importance of wilderness*

✧ ✦ ✧

WATERFALLS

Chelsea House
An imprint of Infobase Publishing
132 West 31st Street
New York NY 10001

ISBN-10: 0-8160-6436-9
ISBN-13: 978-0-8160-6436-6

Library of Congress Cataloging-in-Publication Data
Corrigan, Patricia, 1948–
    Waterfalls / Patricia Corrigan.
        p. cm. — (The extreme earth)
    Includes bibliographical references and index.
    ISBN 0-8160-6436-9
    1. Waterfalls. 2. Folklore—Saparagamuve (Sri Lanka) I. Title. II. Series.
    GB1403.2C66 2006
    551.48'4—dc22   2006001829

Chelsea House books are available at special discounts when purchased in bulk
quantities for businesses, associations, institutions, or sales promotions. Please call
our Special Sales Department in New York at (212) 967-8800 or (800) 322-8755.

You can find Chelsea House on the World Wide Web at http://www.chelseahouse.com

Text design by Erika K. Arroyo
Cover design by Dorothy M. Preston/Salvatore Luongo
Illustrations by Melissa Ericksen and Dale Dyer
Photo research by Diane K. French

Printed in the United States of America

VB SG 10 9 8 7 6 5 4 3 2 1

This book is printed on acid-free paper.

Contents

Foreword

✧✧✧✧✧✧✧✧✧✧✧✧✧✦✧✧✧✧✧✧✧✧✧✧✧✧✧

Waterfalls are unique landforms, far rarer than mountains or valleys, glaciers or lakes. Even the smallest waterfall surprises and delights visitors, but viewing a waterfall is also an opportunity to see geology interact with hydrology as a soft material (in this case, water) sculpts a hard material such as rock.

One of eight titles in the Extreme Earth set, *Waterfalls* presents examples of waterfalls shaped by the powerful forces of tectonic activity, glaciers, volcanism, and erosion. Just as a lake depends on a depression in the ground for it to fill with water, a waterfall depends on an abrupt cliff or escarpment for the water to rush over and tumble down. Compared to the surrounding rock, the cliffs that form the cap rock for waterfalls are harder and more erosion-resistant. Without that harder cap rock, waterfalls cannot form.

The book visits 10 unforgettable locales around the world, describing the power and beauty of the waterfalls as well as their place in history. Studying the examples examined in this book can provide an understanding of how waterfalls develop, age, and even disappear over the span of geologic time. Like any other natural feature in our landscape, waterfalls all are subject to erosion, and some of them may erode quickly enough for changes to be visible in our lifetimes.

Readers likely will be familiar with several of the waterfalls discussed, including Victoria Falls in Zambia and Zimbabwe, named in 1871 by Dr. David Livingstone; Yosemite Falls in California, formed as part of a great glacial valley of the Sierra Nevada; and Niagara Falls, which lies on the border between the United States and Canada. Jog Falls, the tallest waterfall in India, is also discussed here. This once impressive waterfall has been robbed of much of its sustaining waters by a dam used to produce electricity.

As readers will discover in the following pages, some people see waterfalls as economical sources of power and others see them as natural wonders, worthy of preservation. The "In the Field" sections in this book provide details about the methods used by geologists (myself included) and other scientists who study waterfalls. Geologists, biologists, engineers, and archaeologists all study waterfalls—the rocks that form them, the watersheds that provide the water that animates them, the plants and animals that inhabit them, and even the people who have made their homes around them. The book also includes insights into native myths about the creation and meaning of waterfalls in different parts of the world.

Some waterfalls, such as Niagara Falls, are visited by hordes of tourists; others, such as Angel Falls in southeast Venezuela, are far more remote. Lucky readers may live within an easy drive of some of the waterfalls in this book, or they may opt to travel someday to the waterfalls described here. In either case, readers will become more aware of the complexity and features that all waterfalls share. An excellent explanation of the natural processes of waterfalls, *Waterfalls* will help all readers better understand the mechanism—and the majesty—of these impressive and inspiring landforms.

—Geoffrey H. Nash, geologist

Preface

✧✧✧✧✧✧✧✧✧✧✧◆✧✧✧✧✧✧✧✧✧✧✧

From outer space, Earth resembles a fragile blue marble, as revealed in the famous photograph taken by the *Apollo 17* astronauts in December 1972. Eugene Cernan, Ronald Evans, and Jack Schmitt were some 28,000 miles (45,061 km) away when one of them snapped the famous picture that provided the first clear image of the planet from space.

Zoom in closer and the view is quite different. Far beneath the vast seas that give the blue marble its rich hue are soaring mountains and deep ridges. On land, more mountains and canyons come into view, rugged terrain initiated by movement beneath the Earth's crust and then sculpted by wind and water. Arid deserts and hollow caves are here too, existing in counterpoint to coursing rivers, sprawling lakes, and plummeting waterfalls.

The Extreme Earth is a set of eight books that presents the geology of these landforms, with clear explanations of their origins, histories, and structures. Similarities exist, of course, among the many mountains of the world, just as they exist among individual rivers, caves, deserts, canyons, waterfalls, lakes, ocean ridges, and trenches. Some qualify as the biggest, highest, deepest, longest, widest, oldest, or most unusual, and these are the examples singled out in this set. Each book introduces 10 superlative examples, one by one, of the individual landforms, and reveals why these landforms are never static, but always changing. Some of them are internationally known, located in populated areas. Others are in more remote locations and known primarily to people in the region. All of them are worthy of inclusion.

To some people, the ever-shifting contours of the Earth are just so much scenery. Others sit and ponder ocean ridges and undersea trenches, imagining mysteries that they can neither interact with nor examine in person. Some gaze at majestic canyons, rushing waterfalls, or placid lakes, appreciating the scenery from behind a railing, on a path, or aboard a boat. Still others climb mountains, float rivers, explore caves, and cross deserts, interacting directly with nature in a personal way.

Even people with a heightened interest in the scenic wonders of the world do not always understand the complexity of these landforms. The eight books in the Extreme Earth set provide basic information on how individual landforms came to exist and their place in the history of the planet. Here, too, is information on what makes each one unusual, what roles they play in the world today, and, in some cases, who discovered and named them. Each chapter in each volume also includes material on environmental challenges and reports on science in action, with details on field studies conducted at each site. All the books include photographs in color and black-and-white, line drawings, a glossary of scientific terms related to the text, and a listing of resources for more information.

When students who have read the eight books in the Extreme Earth set venture outdoors—whether close to home, on a family vacation, or to distant shores—they will know what they are looking at, how it got there, and what likely will happen next. They will know the stories of how lakes form, how wind and weather work together to etch mountain ranges, and how water carves canyons. These all are thrilling stories—stories that inhabitants of this planet have a responsibility to know.

The primary goal of the Extreme Earth set of books is to inform readers of all ages about the most interesting mountains, rivers, caves, deserts, canyons, waterfalls, lakes, ocean ridges, and trenches in the world. Even as these books serve to increase both understanding of the history of the planet and appreciation for all its landforms, ideally they also will encourage a sense of responsible stewardship for this magnificent blue marble.

Acknowledgments

✧✧✧✧✧✧✧✧✧✧✧✧✦✧✧✧✧✧✧✧✧✧✧✧

Waterfalls was written one drop at a time, and along the way, many people provided unexpected splashes of information and inspiration. I offer here my heartfelt gratitude to them all.

Experts who took time to share their knowledge include G. Donald Bain, Geography Computing Facility, University of California at Berkeley; Julie Bicoy, Director, Molokai Visitors Association; Lee Brown, Ph.D., School of Geology, University of Leeds; Rhyn Davies, Pacific Biodiversity Information Forum; Barbara E. Dunn, Administrative Director, Hawaiian Historical Society; Monica Echeverria, Communications Coordinator, World Wildlife Fund; Mike Ferris, Public Affairs Officer, Columbia River Gorge National Scenic Area; Scott Gediman, Chief, Media & External Relations, Yosemite National Park; Tom Holtey, GeoOdyssey Publications; Allen James, Director of Marketing and Special Events, New York State Office of Parks, Recreation and Historic Preservation; Bob Kimmel, Earth Science Information Center; James B. Layzer, Ph.D., U.S. Geological Survey; Larry Montgomery, Ranger, Yosemite National Park; Diane Nichols, Molokai Visitors Association; Derek Presti, Niagara Falls State Park; P. S. Ranawat, Department of Geology, Mohan Lal Sukhadia University; Carey Tichenor, State Naturalist, Kentucky State Parks; Barry Virgilio, Supervisor, Niagara Region Park Interpretative Program; and Jim F. Wood, Geologic Resources Division, National Park Service.

Individuals who willingly answered specific questions include Shalabh Agarwal, Jérôme Brun, Dean Goss, Torbjorn Hasund, Dominic Hamilton, Angela Kepler, Anne Rudsengen, Pilipo Solatoiro, Bryan Swan, and Gill Zulu.

Professional assistance was kindly provided by Frank Darmstadt, Diane French, Amy L. Conver, Jeanne Hanson, and Geoff Nash. Rocksteady friends who provided moral support include Bill Allen, Debbie Allen, Joan Bray, Philip Coffield, George Durnell, Joan Friedman, and Carl Hoagland. As always, my son, Joel Krauska, was a constant source of encouragement.

Introduction

❖✧✧✧✧✧✧✧✧✧✧✧❖✧✧✧✧✧✧✧✧✧✧✧✧

Roaring over the edge of a cliff where a river comes to an abrupt halt, nestling in rock alcoves, plunging down the side of a mountain—wherever they occur, waterfalls capture attention and the imagination. The initial impression is one of beauty, but look again. In addition to providing a breathtaking scene, water running down rock changes the rock in ways small and large. This book explains why and how that happens and how the waterfalls and the rocks came to be at their present location.

Waterfalls is one volume in a set of books by Chelsea House titled Extreme Earth. These books examine landforms around the world that lend themselves to such superlatives as most unusual, highest, longest, and largest. The focus of *Waterfalls* is 10 waterfalls, each one different and each worthy of attention due to its height, width, power, or geologic history.

These superlative waterfalls, listed here in alphabetical order, include

- Angel Falls in South America
- Cumberland Falls in North America
- Gavarnie Falls in western Europe
- Jog Falls in Asia
- Iguaçu Falls in South America
- Kahiwa Falls in the South Pacific
- Multnomah Falls in North America
- Niagara Falls in North America
- Victoria Falls in Africa
- Yosemite Falls in California

Some of these waterfalls are visible from roadways and some are in remote areas. Angel Falls is the highest waterfall in the world. Yosemite Falls is said to be the highest in the United States. Iguaçu Falls is one of the widest waterfalls in the world. Kahiwa Falls travels down from a sea cliff on the northern edge of a volcanic island that pushed up from the seafloor. Cumberland Falls springs from a coal-rich plateau. Jog Falls, actually four separate cascades, is the subject of a beloved folk song.

Niagara Falls may be the most popular waterfall, as some 14 million people from all over the globe visit it each year. Gavarnie Falls, which flows from an unusual glacial formation, is showcased among a dozen different streams. Victoria Falls has been known for at least 200 years in its country of origin as "the smoke that thunders." Multnomah Falls offers an outstanding opportunity to study age-old geologic formations exposed by erosion.

Each chapter contains details on a specific waterfall, including the location, source, size, volume, and appearance. Material about the geologic makeup and the climate of the area where the waterfall is situated is part of each chapter, as is the history of each waterfall and the people who have lived nearby. Information on recent field studies is also included.

The 10 waterfalls explored in this book represent just a fraction of all the waterfalls of the world. Some are well known and widely admired; others sculpt rock day after day in remote places known to only a few. In the summer of 2005, a wildlife biologist at the Whiskeytown National Recreation Area outside of Redding, California, came upon a 400-foot (121-m) tall waterfall that no one had ever reported seeing. Now known as Whiskeytown Falls, the waterfall (shown in the upper color insert on page C-1) is tucked in a remote part of the 40-year-old recreation area, which covers 43,000 acres (17,401 ha) of wilderness. The three-tiered waterfall tumbles into Crystal Creek.

When word got out about the waterfall, a hiker from Redding said he had visited the site twice in the last 10 years but had kept the place a secret. That same sense of ownership, often bolstered by national or regional pride, sometimes motivates claims of superiority, leading officials in countries the world over to claim they house waterfalls that are the biggest, widest, or most voluminous. Lists of the 10 tallest waterfalls in the world, even those compiled by reputable individuals, are rarely identical. Even those lists that do agree about which waterfall is the tallest, widest, or most powerful may disagree on the exact height, width, or force of the water.

These discrepancies occur for several reasons. Scientists measured some waterfalls 100 years ago or more, made notations, and claimed records. Some of those records are still quoted today, failing to take into consideration changes in the waterfalls. In some instances, standards of measurement may have changed. In others the level of exactitude required by the sources reporting the measurements may vary. Regardless of the cause, confusion is the result, and that confusion leads to a natural hesitancy to present most superlatives as indisputable fact. The *Encyclopaedia Britannica* serves as the source for measurements of individual waterfalls featured in this book.

What is certain is that waterfalls will continue to be discovered—some in areas so remote they cannot be reached (and therefore cannot be measured)—and some waterfalls may never be found. Seclusion, fortunately, does not prohibit grandeur.

Origin of the Landform

Waterfalls

Water falls. Simply put, that is why waterfalls are part of the landscape all over the globe. Gravity is the short answer to the question of why rivers and streams large and small plunge over cliffs, drop to the ground, and then hurry away to connect with the next body of water. The result is one of the most dramatic spectacles of nature.

Waterfalls bring tourists to every area of the globe from Australia to Zimbabwe. Millions of hikers, climbers, kayakers, and nature lovers flock to waterfalls far and near to stand and gape at the sight of streams rushing over cliffs, to hear the roar of the water, and to delight in the spray, as shown in the photograph on page 3. Though chemists insist there is nothing to the popular theory that all those vaporized water molecules are naturally intoxicating, most people remain captivated by the sight, sound, and spray of something wild.

The impact is strongest, of course, in the presence of the most powerful waterfalls, but all waterfalls serve as both artists and engineers of the planet. "Water is the driving force of all nature," wrote Leonardo da Vinci, an artist and engineer who lived in Italy from 1452 to 1519. The formation and structure of waterfalls makes for an interesting story.

HOW WATERFALLS FORM

Waterfalls occur when the flow of a river or stream is abruptly interrupted. Unable to halt at the edge of a cliff or on the side of a mountain, the water plunges down the face of the rock. *Glaciers*—rivers of ice—are responsible for some waterfalls. In prehistoric times, these vast ice rivers gouged out large valleys in mountainous areas, sculpting the land. Yosemite National Park is an example of a glacial valley. Glaciers sometimes formed smaller valleys, called *hanging valleys*, above the large ones. When the ice retreated, tributaries flowing high in the mountains had to drop twice as far to rejoin the river. Bridalveil Fall in Yosemite National Park is a hanging valley waterfall.

Movement deep in the Earth is another cause of waterfalls. When the land shifts, either gradually over thousands of years or abruptly one afternoon, a mountain may either partly collapse or rise up, interrupting a river's flow in the process. Millions of years ago, as a result of movement beneath the crust of the Earth, the peninsula now known as India tilted to the east. Rivers that had previously run east changed direction to flow west, and those bodies of water followed faults and fractures that resulted from the uplifting of the land. Jog Falls, one of many waterfalls in the Western Ghats in southern India, was formed just this way.

All waterfalls, by their nature, are temporary, though as with most changes in the land, alterations take a long time. At the brink, or edge, of each waterfall is *cap rock*, a layer of hard, erosion-resistant rock. Over time the flowing water removes softer layers of rock just under the cap rock. This type of erosion is called an *undercut*. Part of the cap rock, which is more resistant to erosion, eventually weakens and falls to the base of the waterfall. These crushed boulders are called *talus*. Each time the edge of the cap rock shatters, the waterfall recedes upstream, and the slope, or grade, of the rock that supports the waterfall lessens slightly. Over millions of years, the slope dwindles and starts to level out, and the waterfall becomes a simple rapid.

Some scientists predict that eventually Niagara Falls will travel all the way back upstream to Lake Erie and function simply as a rapid. Even rapids change the land. Every body of water carries rocks and rock particles along the path of its channel, and in turn, those particles change each path. Slammed together by the force of the water along the way, these particles, known as *sediment*, bond and form sedimentary rocks. These rocks and other debris carried by the water cause the land to wear away, or erode, and over time erosion may lead to the formation of yet another waterfall.

WATERFALLS AND RIVERS

Many waterfalls occur on young rivers, those rivers in the biggest hurry to reach the sea. A river may exhibit two or more different phases along its course—perhaps having the appearance of an old river at the mouth and a younger river elsewhere. In either case, references to age in regard to rivers refer to a phase of development, not to chronological age. Most waterfalls, including Gavarnie Falls in the Pyrenees Mountains of France, occur in the upper regions of rivers, often located in hills or mountains.

As water hurries along the riverbed, the shape and direction of the channel changes according to the volume of water, or *discharge*, at that place. The fastest streams, those that twist and churn, are said to be in the youthful phase of the river, a time when the flow is concentrated and the stream has few tributaries. These rivers are often characterized by rapids and waterfalls, as shown in the illustration on page 4. Rivers are said to be in early maturity when erosion has reduced the grade of the riverbed. The flow slows as the slope decreases, and the slower the flow, the less sediment it can carry.

Tourists line up along a rock wall at Niagara Falls for a panoramic view of both Horseshoe Falls and the American Falls. (*Patricia Corrigan*)

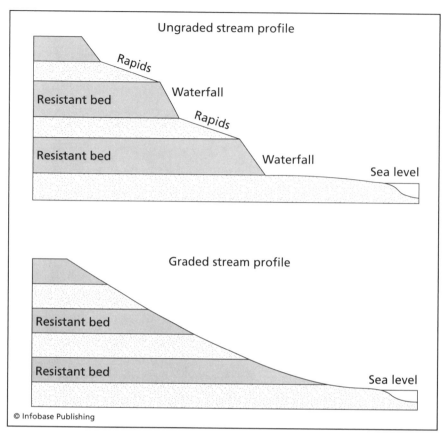

Rivers characterized by rapids and waterfalls have an ungraded profile, while rivers smoothed out by erosion have a graded profile.

Older rivers, made shallower still by a buildup of sediment, have a wider flow. The oldest rivers have broad, flat channels, and their flow proceeds at a pace befitting an elder. That said, even older rivers can pick up speed along the route and reach the ocean sooner rather than later. The Zambezi River has all the characteristics of an older river until it approaches Victoria Falls, located on the border between Zimbabwe and Zambia. There the Zambezi speeds up and sends a huge volume of water racing over the falls.

THE WATER CYCLE

Some waterfalls depend on copious amounts of rain. Others are fed by massive amounts of melting snow. When the snow melts or the rainy season arrives, the water seeks a route over, under, around, or through rock, exerting pressure until the water bursts free. Hours of hard rain, day after day, month after month, add up to enough water to form a significant fall. Angel Falls in Venezuela, the tallest waterfall in the world, is one such

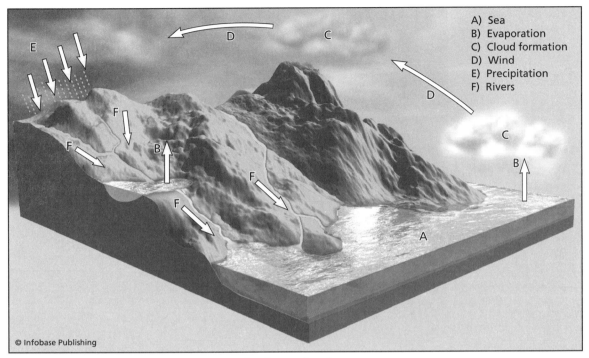

A) Sea
B) Evaporation
C) Cloud formation
D) Wind
E) Precipitation
F) Rivers

© Infobase Publishing

The water cycle, illustrated here, keeps water flowing on the planet.

significant fall. The volume of water is reduced at all waterfalls—even the mighty Angel Falls—in those areas that experience a dry season.

Much of the year, waterfalls have access to a continuing source of water due to the water cycle, a process in nature that keeps water flowing on our planet. As illustrated in the accompanying image, the water cycle works like this: Most rivers go to the sea that is closest by the most direct route. Small bodies of water everywhere drain into larger bodies of water, gathering force at each confluence and eventually flowing into the ocean. The heat of the sun turns water from the oceans into vapor by the process of evaporation. The wind carries the vapor back to the land. When the temperature drops, the vapor condenses. This condensed vapor forms droplets that become clouds, and then drops form that fall as rain. Depending on the condition of the soil, rain either sinks into the ground or flows along the surface. Rainwater falls into flowing streams and rivers and moves with the bodies of water once again to the sea. Then the cycle repeats itself.

WATERFALLS AND POWER PLANTS

Power plants (also known as power stations) are the massive buildings that house the equipment used to produce electricity from water. Power plants often are constructed at the site of large waterfalls. For instance, two power stations, one in the United States and one in Canada, are located just below Niagara Falls. Dams, like the one in the photograph below, are built near power plants to provide reservoirs where water is stored. The water is channeled into long pipes that run from the reservoir to the power station. The force of the water turns the wheels that activate turbines or engines, and the turbines generate electricity known as hydroelectric power.

Harnessing the power of water is not a new concept. In ancient Greece, water powered *gristmills*, mills that ground grain into flour. As early as 610, the Japanese had devised ways to make water do work. The first modern hydroelectric plant was built in 1882 in Appleton, Wisconsin. By 1900, hydroelectric power was used to meet 60 percent of America's power needs. Today about one quarter of the world's electricity is generated by hydroelectric power, and much of that power comes from water diverted from waterfalls.

WATERFALL TERMINOLOGY

In *The Penguin Dictionary of Physical Geography*, author John B. Whittow distinguishes between two types of waterfalls: Cataracts and cascades.

Dams control the flow of water so that power plants may convert the water into electricity. *(James M. Phelps, Jr./www.shutterstock.com)*

Whittow defines a cascade waterfall as "either a small waterfall or a stepped series of small falls or rapids." A cataract waterfall is defined as "a series of stepped waterfalls, generally larger than a cascade, created by a river as it crosses a hard rock band. It is characterised by fast-flowing, broken water which may take the form of rapids (i.e., a staircase of small falls) or merely two or three larger falls. Originally the term was used only to describe a large vertical fall concentrated into a single sheer drop."

Geologists today consider both definitions ambiguous, noting that as defined, a cataract waterfall could be larger in volume, in height, or in width. Other authoritative sources tend to use both terms to describe the same waterfall, and the general public cheerfully uses the terms *cascade* and *cataract* interchangeably. In this book, no attempt will be made to classify waterfalls using these terms.

The late Loren Eisley—a celebrated writer, science educator, teacher, and philosopher who lived from 1907 to 1977—wrote often about the relationship between humans and the natural world. His high regard for waterfalls is evident in this comment: "If there is magic on this planet, it is contained in water."

1

Angel Falls

South America

Angel Falls, the tallest waterfall in the world, tumbles from the top of a rocky cliff in southeast Venezuela on the northern edge of South America. Angel Falls has a total drop of 3,212 feet (979 m). To put that in perspective, the waterfall is almost 20 times higher than Niagara Falls, where the American Falls drops 176 feet (53 m), and almost three times as high as New York City's Empire State Building, which measures 1,250 feet (381 m).

The tallest waterfall in the world (shown in the lower color insert on page C-1) emerges from a canyon in the rugged western range of the Guiana Highlands. Just below the rim of a *mesa*—a flat-topped mountain—the

© Infobase Publishing

Rubble from boulders and rocks above gathers at varying points below a waterfall.

waterfall plunges straight down a breathtaking 2,648 feet (807 m), rarely touching the rock face of the mountain along the way. About 564 feet (171 m) from the base of the falls, the flow is interrupted by *talus*, or rubble from boulders and rocks (as shown in the illustration on page 9) that have fallen from the mountain. The water hurries on and drops at last into a pool at the base of the mountain.

The roar of Salto Ángel, as the waterfall is known throughout South America, can be heard three miles (4 km) away, and the mist and spray, which often shroud the entire cliff, can be seen from great distances. No gauging station measures flow or volume, but Angel Falls boasts an average width of 350 feet (106 m) during the rainy season. At its base, the waterfall is about 500 feet (150 m) wide. In the dry season, from December through April, the stream is much thinner, and Angel Falls's single broad stream sometimes splits into two streams. From June through mid-August, more than a million fish migrate to the area, and many of them congregate at the base of Angel Falls.

TABLETOP MOUNTAINS

Angel Falls tumbles down the face of a mountain known as Auyán-tepuí. In the language of the Pemon, the native Indians in the area, *tepuí* means "mountain." Numerous *tepuís* dot Venezuela's La Gran Sabana, a plain of rolling grasslands, open savannas, and dense forest. All of the *tepuís* are mountains with flat tops, and for that reason, they often are referred to as tabletop mountains. *Tepuís* are characterized by steep, vertical *escarpments*, or cliffs, that feature terraced slopes of jagged rocks. The top of each *tepuí* is riddled with crevices and cracks carved by 102 inches (260 cm) of annual rainfall.

Known locally as Devil's Mountain, Auyán-tepuí is the largest *tepuí* in the state of Bolívar, and one of about 100 such mountains in La Gran Sabana. Towering over a dense, often impenetrable rain forest in Canaima National Park, Auyán-tepuí stands 8,000 feet (2,450 m) high and covers about 434 square miles (1,124 km²).

The tabletop mountains are made up primarily of *sandstone*, rocks formed from the eroded material of igneous, metamorphic, and other rocks. Sandstone is *clastic* sedimentary rock, or a rock made up of fragments of other rocks, bits and pieces left behind where the planet has been battered by wind, water, or ice. This rock waste, caused by weathering, is repeatedly moved about and covered over. Over time, due to the heat and pressure of deep burial, the rock waste solidifies into layers made up of small particles cemented together by minerals that are part of the mix.

Up close, the tabletop mountains are neither flat nor seamless. Meadows of grass or herbs and dwarf forests, most often found along

Vegetation flourishes on the steep tabletop mountains in La Gran Sabana, in the western range of the Guiana Highlands. *(Richard List/CORBIS)*

small streams that course through gullies, cover the surface of the *tepuís*. Eroded rock towers and pinnacles of varying size are equally common, due to fractures and joints in the sandstone. This type of terrain is characterized by *soluble* rock, or rock that can be dissolved and carried away by water.

Like the other tabletop mountains in the western range of the Guiana Highlands, Auyán-tepuí is riddled with cracks and crevices. Those cracks and crevices just below the surface of the plateau catch and hold an abundance of rainwater, a gift from the clouds that drift in from the Atlantic Ocean. Each year the Guiana Highlands receives an annual mean rainfall of 102 inches (260 cm), an amount typical for the tropical climate. The mean annual temperature of La Gran Sabana is 76°F (24.5°C), with temperatures at the summits of the *tepuís* ranging from 46°F (7°C) to 68°F to (20°C).

Beginning in June and continuing into December, rain falls day after day, month after month, swelling the Churun River as it flows atop Auyán-tepuí. Numerous additional streams are created aboveground, and more water pools just below the surface of the tabletop mountains. Seen from the air, some of these streams appear to run gold. Plant tannins provide this coloration. Eventually, all the water collecting atop Auyán-tepuí bursts out of an underground cavern and drops to form the highest waterfall in the world.

DEVIL'S CANYON

At the base of Devil's Mountain is, fittingly enough, Devil's Canyon. There water from Angel Falls and other smaller falls drops into a small creek in the Churun Gorge. That creek then finds its way into the Churun River, which flows into the Carrao River, a tributary of the Caroní River. Eventually, the Caroní travels to meet the Orinoco, which is the third-largest river system in the world.

The source of the Orinoco is at the southern borders of Venezuela and Brazil. The river makes its way west and then north. Then the Orinoco turns east, cutting through Venezuela as it races toward the Atlantic. Grassy planes lie north of the Orinoco. To the south are the tropical forests at the base of the tabletop mountains.

Guri Dam, formally known as the Raúl Leoni Hydroelectric Power Station, is 62 miles (100 km) from the spot where the Caroní River and the Orinoco River meet. Guri Dam is one of the largest dams and *power plants* in the world. Power plants (also known as power stations) house the equipment used to produce electricity from water. The plant at Guri Dam generates 10 million kilowatts of electricity, which supplies power for much of Venezuela. More than 300,000 barrels of oil per day would be required to produce an equivalent amount of energy.

Some 4,300 feet (1,300 m) long and 533 feet (162 m) high, Guri Dam houses two main machine rooms with 10 generators each. Construction on the dam began in 1963. The first of the two machine rooms was finished in 1978, and the second was completed in 1986. Carlos Cruz Diez, a Venezuelan artist, painted designs on the walls in the second machine room. Electrical power is produced as water moving past the dam turns turbines connected to generators. The lake formed by the dam, which boasts an area of 1,513 square miles (3,918 km²), is said to be the second largest in Venezuela. Some recreational facilities are available at the lake, and a new recreation area—Necuima National Park—is under construction.

FORMATION OF THE *TEPUÍS*

The tabletop mountains rest atop the Guiana Shield, a geological formation that extends from Venezuela into Brazil, Guyana, and Colombia. *Shields*, found in the central sections of continents, are considered geologically stable, unlike areas on the edges of continents, known as *mobile belts*, where earthquake and volcanic zones remain active. Shields are among the most ancient rock formations in the world.

A work in progress since the Precambrian Era—which began when Earth first formed some 4.5 billion years ago and ended about 570 million years ago—the Guiana Shield was formed underwater some 1.8 billion years ago from several types of igneous and metamorphic rock. Erosion caused countless layers of compressed sand to build up, forming sandstone.

With the shifting of the continental plates about 200 million years ago, the *tepuís* were lifted and separated, isolating the mountains from one another. Though no elements exist that provide specific clues to date the *tepuís*, geologists have determined that the mountains were in place during the Triassic-Jurassic age, more than 200 million years ago.

Since then, the shape of the *tepuís* has been further refined. Like all landforms, the tabletop mountains continue to change. Waterfalls, of course, are among the change agents at work. Angel Falls is just one of many waterfalls (known as *meru* or *vena* to the Pemon Indians) scattered among the plateaus. These falls—some of them almost half as high as Angel Falls—race down the tall, vertical sides of the *tepuís*. High winds are also characteristic in this region. Working together, the wind and running water continue to gradually alter the landscape.

Bauxite, iron ore, and gold have all been found in the *tepuís*. Bauxite is a naturally occurring material composed primarily of one or more aluminum hydroxide minerals, along with mixtures of silica, iron oxide, titanium, aluminosilicate, and other impurities that occur in minor or trace amounts. Bauxite is the raw material most widely used in the production of *aluminum oxide*, a type of abrasive.

Iron ores are minerals from which metallic iron can be extracted for use in the production of steel. The iron itself is usually found in the form of magnetite or hematite, which are iron oxides. Though iron ores are commonly found throughout the world, much of the pure magnetite and hematite ore has already been mined.

Gold, widely distributed in the Earth's crust, most often occurs in metamorphic rocks and igneous rocks. Though large accumulations of native gold—known more commonly as nuggets—have been found in the area, most often gold occurs as minute grains or in deposits in streams.

CAVES OF THE *TEPUÍS*

The *tepuís* contain more than minerals. In 2002, a Czech-Slovak team of *speleologists*—scientists who study caves—discovered Cueva Ojos de Cristal, or "Cave of the crystal eyes," which measures 7,906 feet (2,410 m) long. This cave is believed to be the fourth-longest and the most-developed *quartzite cave* in the world. A quartzite cave consists

Some quartz crystals have a beveled appearance. (*Dean Allen Caron/www.shutterstock. com*).

of metamorphic rock formed from sandstone that has transformed into *quartz*, an even harder mineral typically found in sandstone or granite. Quartz is the most common of all minerals.

The team found the cave while exploring Mount Roraima, a *tepuí* in the Pacaraima Mountains where the boundaries of Brazil, Venezuela, and Guyana meet. Known locally as "The mother of all waters," Mount Roraima stands 9,094 feet (2,710 m) high and is the highest and most accessible of the *tepuís* in the region. In the May 1989 issue of *National Geographic* magazine, journalist Uwe George wrote this about Mount Roraima: "What I can distinguish of the landscape in the last daylight seems to have come out of a nightmare. Boulders and pinnacles in every size and form are piled one on top of the other. Stormy winds whip ice-cold rain in our faces. There is not one square yard of flat surface. What is not naked, slippery rock is bottomless morass. . . . It is easy to imagine the pinnacles and towers of rock around us as the ruins of temples from strange, long-ago cultures. My mind conjures up colossal Egyptian statues, Greek deities, Siamese pagodas, Roman gods, dwarf elephants, and giant camels—all grown stiff for eternity."

All of the sandstone tabletop mountains, including Mount Roraima, are dotted with numerous *sinkholes*, or depressions in the rock that indicate the presence of caves below. For more than 125 years, speleologists and others have explored Auyán-tepuí, home to Angel Falls. One of the largest *tepuís*, this sandstone mesa is riddled with cracks and crevices, many of which are sinkholes.

In 1993, an expedition conducted by Italian and Venezuelan scientists explored six caves there, including one believed to be the deepest cave in the world that contains rocks consisting of *silica*, the white or colorless crystalline compound of silicone dioxide, which is the composition of the most common mineral group in the world. The cave is almost 1,213 feet (370 m) deep. Geologists say these caves were formed by an underground river system that was in place some 300 million years ago. Some tunnels in the walls of the caves lead to additional caves. The team also explored *simas*, large shafts in the mesa caused by erosion and collapses on the surface. One measured 1,179 feet (360 m) deep, 1,638 feet (500 m) long, and about 327 feet (100 m) wide. Over time the simas will continue to erode.

EARLY STUDIES OF THE *TEPUÍS*

The Pemon Indians, native to the area, have always known about Auyán-tepuí and the other tabletop mountains. Europeans commenced scientific research in the *tepuís* in 1838. Sir Robert Schomburgk, a German naturalist and onetime tobacco farmer in Richmond, Virginia, was the first to study the area, working under the auspices of the Royal Geographical Society of England. In 1884, Everhard Im Thurn and Harry Perkins were the first Europeans to reach the summit of the *tepuís*.

Thurn and Perkins's exhilarating report on Mount Roraima, delivered at a meeting of the Royal Geographical Society, allegedly inspired Sir Arthur Conan Doyle to write a novel about prehistoric animals living on a remote plateau. That book, *The Lost World*, was first published in October 1912, after appearing in serial form in a magazine in March of the same year. The enthusiastic response surpassed all expectations, and Conan Doyle was so enthusiastic about his book that he posed for publicity photos dressed as Professor Challenger, one of the main characters. The book was released as a silent movie in 1925, the first of several versions produced for film and television. The most recent edition of this remarkably successful book was published in 2004.

In 1949, a bold American photojournalist named Ruth Robertson financed and led the first successful overland expedition to the base of Auyán-tepuí. There her team measured the height of Angel Falls, and she declared it to be the world's highest waterfall. Robertson also took the first-known photographs of the falls from the ground. The trip was not easy. History records that Robertson's group had to

---

NAMING RIGHTS

The Pemon Indians call the tallest waterfall in the world Kerepakupai Meru, or "Falls of the deepest place." Why does the rest of the world know a waterfall that plunges down Devil's Mountain into Devil's Canyon as Angel Falls?

The answer may come as a surprise. The name comes from James "Jimmie" Crawford Angel, a bush pilot and adventurer said to be the first westerner to view the "mile-high waterfall." Angel was born in 1899 in Springfield, Missouri. As an adult, he went to work for a mining company based in Tulsa, Oklahoma. Though he was known to be a teller of tall tales, as a pilot Angel quickly gained a reputation for being able to "land on a dime." On a solo flight over Auyán-tepuí in 1933, while looking for gold, Angel caught a glimpse of the waterfall and recorded the sighting in his record book. Not everyone believed him.

Angel wanted another look from a closer vantage point. According to reports published by his niece, Karen Angel, in 1937 Jimmie Angel and a party of four managed to land a plane on top of Auyán-tepuí in hopes of seeing the waterfall. However, the wheels and the nose cone of their plane, El Río Caroní, got stuck in the mud and suffered some damage on landing. Fortunately, during reconnaissance flights before the landing, Angel had dropped a month's worth of supplies, including blankets, flashlights, and food. Stranded at the top of Auyán-tepuí, Angel and his party had no choice but to walk down to the valley below. The trip took 11 days.

Months later the buzz about Angel's trip to find the waterfall still had not abated. Under the most casual of circumstances, Angel's friends and coworkers decided to name the falls after the bush pilot, and the name stuck.

For 27 years, Angel's plane sat in the mud atop Auyán-tepuí. In 1964, the Venezuelan Air Force removed the El Río Caroní from the top of the mountain and took it to an aviation museum for restoration. Today the plane is on display in front of the passenger terminal of Ciudad Bolívar Airport, which is about 160 miles (260 km) southeast of Angel Falls. Jimmie Angel died in Panama in 1956 after a plane crash. His body was cremated, and friends scattered his ashes over Angel Falls.

---

carry heavy equipment along dry rivers and through dense rain forest on the final leg of the journey leading to the base of Auyán-tepuí. Later Robertson wrote an article about the expedition for *National Geographic* magazine titled "Jungle Journey to the World's Highest Waterfall." The article was published in the November 1949 issue of the magazine.

FLORA AND FAUNA OF THE *TEPUÍS*

Four different vegetation zones exist on each *tepuí*: the base, the terraced slope leading to the escarpment, the base of the escarpment, and the summit. Some 2,300 species of plants—including 500 different species of orchids—exist in the region, 766 of them *endemic*, or native. A total of 65 plants, including 20 species of bamboos, are found only on the Guiana Shield.

On the summit, trees—many of them dwarfed due to high winds—grow most often near streams. *Carnivorous* plants, also known as insect-eating plants, grow in shaded crevices or on bluffs, in open savanna, and in sandy or rocky areas. At the base of the mountains, hardy plants live either on bare sandstone or in cracks. Humid cloud forests populate the rocky slopes that lead up to the base of the cliffs, where grassy savanna and rain forests, some with canopies as high as 147 feet (44 m), are located.

Most of the 186 mammal species that live on the *tepuís* make their homes on the lower slopes. The mammals include nine primates (among them howler monkeys), five cats (including jaguars, ocelots, and pumas) and several rodents (among them three climbing rats and two species of guinea pigs). Opossums, weasels, and bats also make their home in the area.

More than 628 birds are found in the region, including ospreys, broad-winged hawks, parakeets, and swifts. The slopes and summits of the *tepuís* are home to numerous snakes, including the highly venomous fer-de-lance. Other snakes typically found include the coral snake, boa constrictor, and bushmaster. Iguanas and lizards are common in the area.

CANAIMA NATIONAL PARK

Auyán-tepuí is located in Canaima National Park, which spreads over some 11,600 square miles (30,043 km²). The park is located in the Piar and Roscio districts of the state of Bolívar in southeast Venezuela. Altitudes in the park range from 1,148 feet (350 m) to 8,858 feet (2,700 m). The borders of the park extend from the Carrao River and the Lema Mountain Range in the north to the Pacaraima Mountain Range all the way to the Brazilian border in the south. The eastern border runs along the headwaters of the Venamo River and the Roraima Mountains across to the Caroní River in the west. Ciudad Bolívar, the nearest city, is 372 miles (600 km) north of Canaima National Park.

The park was founded in 1962, and the size was doubled some 13 years later. Canaima National Park contains three distinctly different terrains: lowlands in the northwestern part of the park, the flat plateau of the La Gran Sabana, and the tabletop mountains. In 1994, the park was added to the list of Natural World Heritage Sites by the United Nations Educational, Scientific and Cultural Organization.

IN THE FIELD: IMPROVING CONSERVATION EFFORTS

An estimated 10,000 *indigenous*, or native, Pemon live in Canaima National Park, home of Auyán-tepuí and Angel Falls. Most of these individuals live in the eastern sector of the park, in communities of between 40 and 100 people. Many of them maintain traditional lifestyles, though they have access to drinking water, electricity, schools, and basic medical care.

Though Canaima National Park prohibits the extraction of natural resources within its boundaries, the Pemon clear small plots in the forests and cultivate the land. Over time the soil runs out of nutrients. Then the Pemon cut down more forest and begin again. This slash-and-burn system has resulted in a fragile ecosystem damaged by fire, the depletion of game and fish, pollution, mining, and logging.

In conjunction with other like-minded agencies, the Nature Conservancy is working to encourage the Pemon to consider a shift from agriculture to ecotourism, a move that will help accommodate their growing population and protect their homeland as well. The Nature Conservancy is an international, nonprofit organization dedicated to preserving the diversity of life on Earth by protecting the lands and waters that plants and animals need to survive.

Working in partnership in Venezuela with the Nature Conservancy are the following organizations: EcoNatura, the Venezuelan National Institute of Parks (INPARQUES), National Experimental University of Guayana, and the National General Directorate of Indigenous Affairs of the Education, Culture and Sports Ministry. The conservation organizations are conducting a study of the impact of tourism on Canaima National Park. Other projects include training members of the Pemon community in nature tourism and adventure tourism. The compatible goals of these projects are to improve the local economy while avoiding overuse of the park's natural resources.

THE FUTURE OF ANGEL FALLS

All of the *tepuís* in the western range of the Guiana Highlands are protected under Venezuelan law as national monuments. Access to the mountains, and to Angel Falls itself, requires a four-day boat trip along rivers bordered by thick jungle. Indeed, because the *tepuís* are so isolated, some writers have described them as "ecological islands." Isolation, though, has not guaranteed complete protection.

Hikers and campers who have made their way through the dense forest have damaged vegetation on the summits and at the bases of some *tepuís* with campfires, and some of those individuals have also left behind litter. Mining for gold and diamonds, which is illegal, has also caused some damage to the land. Because of the sandy quality of the soil, vegetation does not recover quickly. Also, a small population of native hunters threatens the continuation of some species of mammals and birds.

That said, Auyán-tepuí and the other tabletop mountains have little to fear from encroaching civilization. Remote and inaccessible, much of this inhospitable area remains unexplored, and that may ensure the future of Angel Falls, the tallest waterfall in the world.

2

Victoria Falls

Africa

The wide, easygoing Zambezi River runs through six countries, flowing some 1,677 miles (2,700 km) through south-central and southeastern Africa. The river moves peacefully along until a certain point just above the border between Zambia and Zimbabwe. There the Zambezi picks up speed, and then suddenly drops 355 feet (108 m) into a mile-wide (2 km) gorge that separates the nations. This roaring, hissing torrent of water is Victoria Falls.

Victoria Falls stretches 5,500 feet (1,700 m) long and produces an average volume of 246,857 gallons (934,455 L) of water per second. The broad curtain of falling water is twice as high and one-and-a-half times as wide as Niagara Falls. Close to the falls, numerous small islands interrupt the course of the Zambezi. The islands divide the river into a series of channels that drop in many separate falls.

The four major cascades that make up Victoria Falls are:

- Devil's Cataract
- Main Falls
- Rainbow Falls
- Eastern Cataract

Devil's Cataract is 88 feet (27 m) wide and 196 feet (60 m) high. A large rock juts out from the center of Main Falls, causing water to pour down on either side from a height of 272 feet (83 m). Respective widths of the two cascades are 1,719 feet (524 m) and 974 feet (297 m). Rainbow Falls is 1,804 feet (550 m) wide and 328 feet (100 m) high, and the Eastern Cataract measures 997 feet (304 m) wide and 314 feet (96 m) high.

Some 23–27 inches (600–700 mm) of rain falls annually, and the Zambezi River typically floods in February and March. During flood season, Victoria Falls reaches a maximum volume of 1,870,129 gallons (7,079,208 L) of water per second. In the spring, the spray—visible from miles away—rises in the air as high as 1,650 feet (502 m). The spray often completely

Numerous small islands interrupt the flow of the Zambezi River as it approaches Victoria Falls. *(Bertie Coetzee/www.shutterstock.com)*

obscures the falls. As seen in the upper color insert on page C-2, on sunny days colorful rainbows form in the clouds of mist that rise from Victoria Falls. The mean annual temperature at Victoria Falls is 68°F (20°C).

THE MANY NAMES OF THE FALLS

The unbridled power generated by Victoria Falls creates plenty of smoke and thunder. Two native tribes—the Makalolo and the Lozi—have been credited with naming the falls Mosi-oa-Tunya, or "Smoke that thunders." An earlier name, similar in theme, comes courtesy of the Ndebele tribe. They called the falls Amanza Thunquayo, or "Water rising as smoke." The rest of the world knows this dramatic landform as Victoria Falls.

David Livingstone, the first European to see the waterfall, named it for England's Queen Victoria. A Scottish missionary and explorer, Livingstone was traveling in the area in November 1855. Legend has it that he spent a night on an island upstream from the falls. He set off the next morning in a dugout canoe navigated by natives. The party landed on a second island just above the falls, and from there Livingstone had a superlative view of massive amounts of water pouring into the gorge. The island is now known as Livingstone Island.

Recalling that first good look, Livingstone wrote, "Creeping with awe to the verge, I peered down into a large rent which had been made from bank to bank of the broad Zambezi, and saw that a stream of a thousand yards broad leaped down a hundred feet and then became suddenly compressed into a space of fifteen to twenty yards."

Livingstone proclaimed the falls "the most wonderful sight I had witnessed in Africa." His description of the surrounding area was eloquent: "No one can imagine the beauty of the view from anything witnessed in England. It had never been seen before by European eyes, but scenes so lovely must have been gazed upon by angels in their flight."

FORMATION OF THE FALLS

When a cataclysmic shift in the Earth occurred some 2 million years ago, the upper Zambezi River abandoned its southeasterly direction and headed east to flow over layers of *sandstone* and *basalt*. Sandstone is sedimentary rock formed from the eroded material of igneous, metamorphic, and other sedimentary rocks. Sediment is a form of rock waste, bits and pieces left behind where the planet has been battered by wind, water, or ice. This rock waste, caused by weathering, is repeatedly moved about and covered over. Over time it solidifies into layers made up of small grains cemented together (due to heat and pressure) by minerals that are part of the mix.

The most common form of lava is basalt, an *extrusive igneous rock*, which means that the rock quickly crystallized from liquid magmas that reached the surface and then were generally vented as volcanic lavas. Basalt is dark, fine-grained, and heavy. The bed of basalt under the Zambezi is about 1,000 feet (305 m) thick. Archaeologists have found numerous crude prehistoric tools in the area, which they believe were fashioned

DAVID LIVINGSTONE

David Livingstone first explored Africa in the hope of opening trade routes while doing missionary work. *(Library of Congress)*

David Livingstone, born March 19, 1813, perhaps is best known as the man Henry Morton Stanley was sent to find in the African wilderness. Livingstone, who had gone to Africa searching for the source of the Nile River, was thought to be lost—if not dead. An editor at the *New York Herald* sent Stanley, a 28-year-old newspaper reporter, to Africa as a publicity stunt. Even the reporter's name was a scam. Stanley's real name was John Rowlands.

In March 1871, Stanley bought supplies, hired porters, and left Zanzibar to head into the African interior. The trip was not easy. Over a six-month period, members of the search party endured floods and drought and were ill more often than not. On November 10, Stanley finally arrived in Ujiji, on the shores of Lake Tanganyika. Livingstone, 51, pushed through a crowd surrounding Stanley, who supposedly intoned, "Dr. Livingstone, I presume?" Livingstone replied in the affirmative.

Born in a small village in Scotland, Livingstone studied medicine and theology at the University of Glasgow. He then moved to London, where he joined the London Missionary Society. During a four-year stint in what is now Botswana, Livingstone was credited with converting one person to Christianity. From 1852 to 1856, he traveled across Africa in hopes of opening trade routes. He returned to England in 1856 to publish a book on his travels and gain support for exploring the Zambezi River.

Back in Africa some years later, Livingstone and his team discovered that a key part of the river could not be navigated past a series of rapids that he had failed to explore on his earlier travels. The team broke up. Some died, some resigned, and some were fired. Livingstone stayed in Africa until 1864, when he returned home in hopes of raising more money for further exploration. Two years later, he returned to Africa, charged with determining whether the source of the Nile was Lake Albert or Lake Victoria, a question of fierce debate in England. (The correct answer is Lake Albert.)

Though Livingstone's health began to deteriorate, he continued to explore. When he happened upon the Lualaba River, a tributary of the Congo River that was farther west in Africa than any European had traveled, Livingstone insisted that the river actually was the Nile.

After Stanley "found" Livingstone, the two explored what is now Tanzania. At the time, Livingstone was in poor health. Stanley left the country in 1872, and the following year, on May 1, 1873, Livingstone died in Zambia. Two of his longtime attendants carried Livingstone's body for more than 1,000 miles (1,609 km) so that it might be returned to Britain. Livingstone is buried in Westminster Abbey in London.

from chunks of the soft basalt. Cleavers and axes, as well as a six-sided weapon, have also been found.

The Zambezi River travels about 129 miles (209 km) over the basalt and sandstone plateau, which is riddled with faults and cracks that developed as the molten lava cooled. Geologists report zones of soft material within the basalt, including a dominant series of *joints* that run east and west. These zones of soft material in the rock are responsible for the formation of the waterfall, as shown in the illustration below. Over time the Zambezi River cut through the soft material in the joints and fractures to form the deep, narrow gorge that now showcases Victoria Falls.

PREVIOUS FALLS

The gorge that receives the crashing water delivered by the Zambezi River is not the first site of a major waterfall in this area. A series of seven

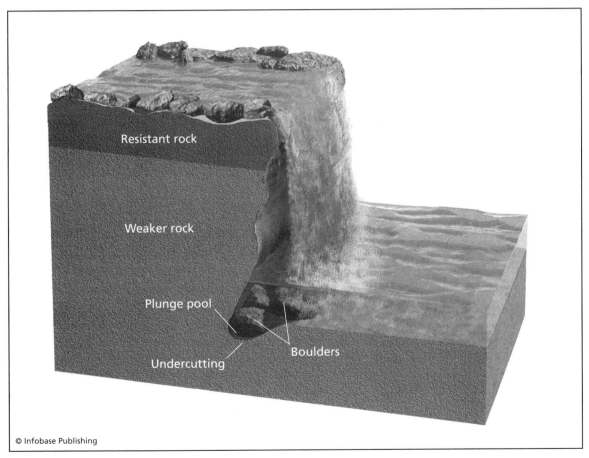

© Infobase Publishing

This drawing illustrates a river plunging down the face of a cliff to form a waterfall.

zigzagging gorges that were carved out downstream where the river once ran represent seven previous waterfalls, each similar in size to Victoria Falls. The farthest is 4.9 miles (8 km) from the current falls.

In other words, on seven different occasions, the gradual erosion of faults and joints that run perpendicular to the Zambezi caused the river to drop into a narrow fissure before reaching the existing falls, a process called vertical river erosion. As the narrow gorge deepened, the water eventually pushed through another zone of soft material in the sandstone and basalt. Rock tumbled into the gorge, the water dropped, and a new, broad fall was established.

The process continues. Due to a second major series of cracks that run north and south in the riverbed, the Zambezi River will gradually retreat upstream. On the Zimbabwe side, Devil's Cataract (shown in the photograph on page 25) already is lower than the rest of the falls by 68 to 121 feet (21 to 37 m). That difference in height indicates that the water is beginning to cut back along a weak line in the rock. Over time this continuous gradual erosion will result in a new line of falls.

FANS OF THE FALLS

David Livingstone was one of many fans of Victoria Falls, a landform that continues to evoke superlatives from visitors to this day. Frederick C. Selous was a British game hunter, soldier, and legendary pioneer of Africa. Selous Game Reserve in Tanzania is named for him. In 1881, Selous penned these words about Victoria Falls:

> At whatever part one looks, the rays of the sun shining on the descending masses of foam form a double zone of prismatic colors, of whose depth and brilliancy no one who has only seen the faint tints of an ordinary rainbow can form any conception. Such are the Victoria Falls—one of, if not the most transcendentally beautiful natural phenomenon on this side of Paradise.

Selous and Livingstone left their mark at Victoria Falls in another way as well. Both are said to have carved their names on tree trunks on numerous islands along the river, including the one later named for Livingstone.

Jumbo Williams, a photographer, followed the modern-day trend of taking only photos and leaving only footprints. However, after paying written tribute, he also expressed a more phobic appreciation of Victoria Falls than either Livingstone or Selous.

"The first impression was unmistakable; immense power, the raw energy unleashed when the entire Zambezi leaps wildly into a black two kilometer [1.24-mile-] wide abyss. The scale is massive, the spectacle spellbinding and perpetually changing," Williams wrote in his book *Zambezi, River of Africa*, published in 1988. Williams continues: "The falls hiss and roar as if possessed, they rumble and crash like thunder. Vast clouds spew and billow out from the seething cauldron of its dark impenetrable depths. The moving water creates a magnetism that sucks you closer, so that you recoil in horror to quench a subliminal sacrificial urge."

At 196 feet (60 m), Devil's Cataract is lower than the rest of Victoria Falls. *(Marco Alegria/www.shutterstock.com)*

The spray from Victoria Falls nourishes a 14-square-mile (23-km²) rain forest atop the cliff just across the gorge. This rain forest represents a fragile ecosystem built on an accumulation of sandy sediment. Several species of trees grow in the forest, including acacia, ebony, mahogany, ivory palm, African olive, date palm, and at least two different types of fig trees. Numerous ferns and flowers also grow in the forest. The ecosystem is dependent on the humidity resulting from the ever-present mist produced by the falls.

VICTORIA FALLS NATIONAL PARK

Spread over seven square miles (18 km²), Victoria Falls National Park comprises the western half of Victoria Falls—the heart of the park—and a stretch of the Zambezi River for several miles below the falls. The park lies on the western edge of Matabeleland North Province (Hwange District) on the southern bank of the Zambezi River. The park shares borders with Zambezi National Park and the Matetsi-Kazuma Pan-Hwange complex in Zimbabwe and Mosi-oa-Tunya National Park in Zambia.

In 1935, the government of Zimbabwe declared Victoria Falls a national monument. Two years later, officials set aside the Victoria Falls Reserve, an area extending five miles (8 km) from the falls, for governance by the Historic Monument Commission. In 1952, this reserve was combined with the Victoria Falls Game Reserve to form Victoria Falls National Park.

Seven years later, the park was subdivided once again, to form Victoria Falls National Park and Zambezi National Park. The latter covers 2,485 square miles (6.436 km²) on the Zambian bank of the river. In 1970, national monument status was extended to all of Victoria Falls National Park. Well over half of the park was declared a World Heritage Site in 1989 by the United Nations Educational, Scientific and Cultural Organization.

HUMAN POPULATION AT VICTORIA FALLS

The population just outside Victoria Falls National Park is made up of recent immigrants and long-term occupants. The Tonga people have lived in the area the longest, for seven centuries or more. Other tribes in the area include the Subiya, Leya, Toka, and Totela. Smaller numbers of Nanzwa, Yeyi, and Mbukushu have a long history of living in the area. More recent immigrants include the Lozi, Kololo, Ndebele, and numerous English-speaking individuals.

Most park visitors stay in the nearby town of Victoria Falls in Zimbabwe, which is accessible by road, rail, or air. Paths are available from the town through the rain forest that leads to the falls. One-third of the way down the gorge, there is a viewing platform. The Victoria Falls Bridge, which crosses the gorge some 364 feet (111 m) above the Zambezi, is another spot that provides views of the gorge in one direction and Victoria Falls in the other.

FAUNA AT VICTORIA FALLS

More than 30 species of mammals live in Zambezi National Park, which shares a border with Victoria Falls National Park. Among them are elephants, Cape buffalo, hippos, rhinos, and lions. Other animals found in the area include wildebeests, giraffes, zebras, warthogs, baboons, vervet monkeys, and bush pigs. Common antelope species include waterbuck, kudu, bushbuck, impala, eland, and klipspringer. Because of the plentiful wildlife, Victoria Falls is something of a gateway for tourists eager to see—and photograph—Africa's legendary wildlife, though the parks are not yet set up to accommodate visitors as handily as some other parks in Kenya and Tanzania.

Some 400 species of birds live in the Victoria Falls region, with differing populations in the gorges, the rain forest, and the woodland areas. Species include the fish eagle, black stork, augur buzzard, martial eagle, trumpeter hornbill, black-cheeked lovebird, Egyptian and Knobilled goose, and the common African skimmer. Scientists say all species are suffering from human disturbance (boats and trains) and bush clearance.

Reptile species in the area are also declining. The python is the largest snake in the area, where most of the snakes are nonvenomous. Two species of tortoise live in the Zambezi River, as do lizards, skinks and chameleons. Frogs and toads are present in abundance, as are some 84 species of fish.

Parks and wildlife scientists monitor all animals and plants at Victoria Falls National Park and Zambezi National Park. Environmental research is conducted through the Zambezi-Matetsi complex, with laboratories at Isidumuka, some 55 miles (89 km) south of Victoria Falls.

THE ZAMBEZI RIVER

The Zambezi River—the fourth largest in Africa after the Nile, Zaire, and Niger Rivers—begins its 1,677-mile (2,700-km) journey as a small spring in northwestern Zambia. The spring is said to bubble up from between the roots of a tree not far from the point where Zambia, Angola, and Zaire share a border.

The river flows through Angola, where it picks up significant drainage from other rivers. Then the Zambezi reenters Zambia, flowing south and increasing once again in size as the result of connecting tributaries. Traveling through Zambia, the river runs through flat, sandy country, crosses a broad plain, and then flows through rock-laden country that houses a series of rapids and the Ngonye Falls.

Some 186 miles (300 km) upriver from Victoria Falls is Ngonye Falls. Also known as Sioma Falls, the horseshoe-shaped falls is near a town of the same name in western Zambia. Crescent-shaped, Ngonye Falls is only 32–82 feet (10–25 m) high, but it is said to boast an impressive width. Here the Zambezi flows underneath the rock on either side of the falls, and visitors who make their way to these remote and nearly inaccessible falls report feeling and hearing the underground flow when standing above the falls.

Just above Ngonye Falls, the Zambezi leaves the Kalahari sand floodplain to travel over basalt. The geological process that resulted in Victoria Falls—erosion of cracks in the basalt riverbed—is the same process that formed Ngonye Falls. Historians report that David Livingstone saw Ngonye Falls before he viewed Victoria Falls.

Turning east the Zambezi forms the border between Zambia and Namibia. Farther along, in partnership with the Chobe River, the Zambezi forms a border along Botswana for a brief distance. The Zambezi then serves as the border between Zambia and Zimbabwe, traveling some 310 miles (500 km) between the countries. After making a dynamic impression as it plunges over Victoria Falls, the river winds through the narrow Batoka Gorge, with walls ranging from 400 to 750 feet (121 to 228 m) deep. Eventually, the gorge gives way to a broad valley.

The river travels north for a time and then shifts to the east. At Chirundu, the Lower Zambezi National Park (on the Zambian side) and Mana Pools National Park (on the Zimbabwean side) flank the river, which supports this important wilderness area. The Luangwa River then joins the Zambezi, flowing first into Mozambique and then to the Indian Ocean.

FESTIVAL ON THE RIVER

The town of Mungo in western Zambia, upriver from Victoria Falls, is the site of an annual festival known as Ku-omboka. Typically, the festival is held at the end of the rainy season, usually in late March or early April. Thousands of people move to higher ground when the Zambezi floods. ("Ku-omboka" literally translates as "To get out of the water onto dry ground.")

The Lozi chief and his family are the focal point of Ku-omboka, which is said to be one of the last great public ceremonies in southern Africa. Attired in traditional dress, men steer massive canoes from the chief's palace at Lealui down the Zambezi to Limulunga—a six-hour journey—where a royal residence sits on higher ground, safe from flooding. The Lozi people follow their chief, and once all have arrived, everyone sings and dances in celebration.

IN THE FIELD: LIGHTING VICTORIA FALLS

In 2004, an ambitious plan to light Victoria Falls at night came under fire from environmentalists. In preparation for a tourism campaign titled "Visit Zambia 2005," the Zambian government, working with the Zambia Electricity Supply Corporation (ZESCO), proposed repairing six vandalized electric lamps and supplying electricity to them so that tourists might enjoy the waterfall after dark. (The lights had not been in use since 1989.) Environment Africa, a nature organization based in Zimbabwe, was among the groups opposed to the plan. Opponents of the measure went so far as to suggest that the United Nations might drop Victoria Falls from the list of World Heritage Sites if the plan was carried out. Citing a UNESCO policy regarding development at the site, analysts proposed an environmental impact assessment to determine whether lighting the falls would affect the traditional values of the site. The Zambia National Tourist Board countered that the lights should be in place until results of such an assessment were released. Meanwhile, the Ministry of Tourism, Environment and Natural Resources began negotiations with the governments of Zambia and Zimbabwe.

The lights were repaired and, eventually, lit. Early in 2005, the Environmental Council of Zambia issued a ruling that Victoria Falls may not be lit and instructed ZESCO to switch off the lights once and for all. The council noted that the Zambia National Tourist Board had acted illegally by restoring the lights before completion of the environmental impact assessment. As of April 2006, no deadline had been set for that assessment.

AN ECONOMIC BOON

Victoria Falls has faced other threats. Several years ago, Zimbabwe considered building a dam on the Zambezi River where it winds through the Batoka Gorge, just 34 miles (56 km) from Victoria Falls. Government officials in favor of the plan said they were searching for a source of reliable electricity generation.

The dam currently closest to Victoria Falls is Kariba Dam. Located in the Kariba Gorge on the Zambezi River between Zambia and Zimbabwe, Kariba Dam is 250 miles (400 km) from Victoria Falls. Lake Kariba—the dam's 175-mile (280-km)-long reservoir—covers about 2,000 square miles (5,179 km²). Just after Lake Kariba was filled in 1963, an earthquake occurred under the lake that measured 5.8 on the Richter scale. Since then, numerous additional earthquakes have occurred in the area, 20 of them rated in excess of magnitude 5. Engineers and seismologists cannot say exactly why these quakes have occurred, but seismograph stations, designed to detect vibrations in the ground, have been installed in the region.

The first stage of the concrete arch dam at Kariba Dam—said to be one of the largest in the world—was constructed between 1955 and 1959, and the second part was completed in 1977. The total cost was $480 million. Measuring 419 feet (128 m) high and 1,899 feet (579 m) long, the *power plant* at Kariba Dam generates 1,320 megawatts of electricity, serving areas in both Zambia and Zimbabwe. Power plants, also called power stations, house the machines that generate electricity from water.

The plan to build a dam in the Batoka Gorge was recently shelved for financial reasons, but officials were also concerned when studies investigating the potential of such a dam revealed that future climate change might cause "significant reductions" in the river flow. Reductions in flow would likely mean a decline of the hydropower that was originally intended to offset the effects of climate change.

Tourism groups were much relieved when the dam project was shelved. Had the Batoka Gorge Dam been built, an area of rapids known for whitewater rafting would have been inundated, effectively bringing to an end the opportunities for commercial tourism now in place at Victoria Falls. Tourism at the falls is important to Zambia and Zimbabwe, countries with significant economic and political problems. Both countries benefit greatly because a world-renowned river makes a steep drop between their borders, forming the magnificent Victoria Falls.

3 ✧✧✦✧✧✦✧✧✦✧✧✦✧✧✦✧✧✦✧✧✦✧✧✦✧

Yosemite Falls

North America

A breathtaking natural spectacle amid the landscape of spectacles that is Yosemite National Park, Yosemite Falls rushes down from a cleft in a high granite cliff. That cliff and the surrounding mountains are part of the western Sierra Nevada in central California. Said to be the highest freefalling waterfall in North America and the fifth tallest in the world, Yosemite Falls plunges 2,425 feet (739 m) into Yosemite Valley.

As a point of comparison, Yosemite Falls is equal to the combined heights of the Sears Tower in Chicago and the Eiffel Tower in Paris. This dramatic waterfall consists of three parts:

- Upper Yosemite Fall, which measures 1,430 feet (436 m)
- Middle Cascade, which drops 675 feet (205 m)
- Lower Yosemite Fall, which measures 320 feet (98 m)

The roar of the falls reverberates through Yosemite Valley, and great quantities of spray and mist rise up from the *talus*, a pile of crushed boulders, at the base of Yosemite Falls.

The interruption in the flow of the falls is due to two ledges, both overgrown with brush, that jut out from the vertical cliff walls. The ledges formed as a result of two horizontal joint systems, or groups of linear cracks in the granite. One joint system is near the base of the Upper Fall and the other is near the brink of the Lower Fall.

YOSEMITE CREEK

Yosemite Falls is fed by Yosemite Creek. High above the floor of Yosemite Valley, Yosemite Creek springs from Grant Lake and then travels over a rolling plateau of mostly barren granite. Along the course, few lakes are in the area to compete with the creek for water storage. Below Yosemite Falls, Yosemite Creek flows into the Merced River, which moves through Yosemite Valley. The Merced travels southwest through the foothills and across the San Joaquin Valley. The river then joins the San Joaquin River, which later forms a large delta with the Sacramento River, the longest river in California, with a length of 382 miles (614 km). The river eventually flows into the north arm of San Francisco Bay.

Each year heavy snowmelt swells Yosemite Creek, causing Yosemite Falls to thunder at maximum volume from late winter through early to midsummer. The lower color insert on page C-2 illustrates the peak flow in mid-April. A gauging station to provide accurate flow measurements does not exist, but *hydrologists*, scientists who study water, estimate an average spring flow of 2,400 gallons (9,000 L) per second. At peak flow, each drop of water traveling at 12 miles (19 km) per hour takes just three minutes to make the journey from the top of the falls to the bottom.

By late summer, the roar of Yosemite Falls has quieted to a whisper, and sometimes it dries up completely. In early winter, an ice cone typically forms at the base of Upper Yosemite Fall. Officials have recorded the maximum height of the cone at 322 feet (98 m), which is about as tall as a 25-story building. In early spring, water rushing down from the Upper Fall pierces the top of the cone. By mid-April, the last of the cone has melted. The ice cone, an annual occurrence, and the heavy flow of water in the spring have helped to carve the recessed alcoves that frame Yosemite Falls and other waterfalls in Yosemite National Park.

Cliff recession, a form of erosion, also plays a part in formation of the alcoves. Sheer cliffs typically form where a series of linear cracks in the granite cause rock to flake off the cliff, continuing to expose nearly vertical surfaces. Geologists report that the cliffs surrounding Yosemite Falls have receded significantly since glacial times.

HANGING VALLEY

Yosemite Falls occurs in a *hanging valley*, a valley that forms a cliff face above the main valley because the lower part has been eroded. A geologic process known as *differential erosion* created the hanging valley. Differential erosion, which occurs at varying rates, due to the differences in the resistance of surface materials, took place when glaciers and powerful rivers moving through what is currently Yosemite Valley sculpted a deep, U-shaped gorge from what had been a gentle V-shaped canyon. This transformation of the valley left Yosemite Creek and other tributaries with no choice but to drop further distances into the valley.

Differential erosion occurred for several reasons. The upstream watershed was originally larger and provided more water for the rivers and more ice for the glaciers. These rivers and glaciers also flowed down the western Sierran slope, which allowed for more speed and more erosive power. (Tributaries flowing in from the north or south are relatively less steep, as they flow across the western slope.) Third, the granite undergoing erosion contained cracks or joints that ran east and west, the same general direction as the flowing rivers and glaciers. These cracks gave way more readily, allowing for more extensive erosion.

YOSEMITE VALLEY

Yosemite Valley measures seven miles (11 km) long and one mile (1.6 km) across at its widest point, as seen in the upper color insert on page C-3. The valley was carved out during three different glacial periods, though this was not always common knowledge. According to William R. Jones, writing in *Domes, Cliffs and Waterfalls: A Brief Geology of Yosemite Valley*, the early Miwok Indians imagined that the granite cliffs were "rocks that grew and people turn to stone." Josiah Whitney, a geology professor at Harvard University, opined in 1865 that Half Dome had been "split asunder, the lost half having gone down in the rack of the matter and the crush of worlds." John Muir, a sheepherder turned naturalist, figured out

Half Dome, in Yosemite National Park, is rounded on three sides and flattened on the fourth. *(Patricia Corrigan)*

Naturalist John Muir, writing in 1890, described Yosemite Valley as "a temple lighted from above." *(George Grantham Bain Collection/Library of Congress)*

that ice had sculpted the land, a theory confirmed in 1930 by geologist and surveyor François Matthes.

Some 2 to 3 million years ago, the ice field that formed along the crest of the Sierra Nevada periodically generated *glaciers*, or rivers of ice, that under the force of gravity moved down into the steep, narrow canyons that the rivers had created. Vast quantities of snow and ice accumulated in these valleys, sometimes at a depth of up to 3,000 feet (914 m).

Amid the snow and ice was every scrap of rock and rubble the glaciers had collected along the way. Grinding along, gouging out more rock from the granite walls that lined the valley, the gigantic, powerful glaciers changed the landscape, carving sloped valleys into U-shaped troughs, fashioning jagged peaks, and dotting the area with lakes. Some of the granite was polished, rather than removed or reshaped, and much of the rock debris, abandoned in streams and rivers as the glaciers melted, now lies scattered across the landscape of central northern California.

At one time, the entire valley was covered by a deep lake that formed as glaciers receded. Due to natural climate changes, the lake filled with *sediment*, particles of rock and debris discarded by receding glaciers. The water dried up, plants took hold, meadows developed, and some of those meadows produced forests. This process is known as *succession*, now in evidence at Mirror Lake in Tenaya Canyon, just above the head of Yosemite Valley.

ROCK FORMATIONS

Only the sheetlike granite walls sturdy enough to withstand the immense pressure of the glaciers remained in place. Today the world knows two of these massive cliffs as El Capitan and Half Dome. El Capitan, a sheer cliff some 3,593 feet (1,095 m) high, is said to be the largest granite *monolith*, or large block of stone, in the world. Half Dome (shown in the photograph on page 32), is rounded on three sides and flat on the fourth and rises over 4,733 feet (1,443 m) above the floor of Yosemite Valley.

Other famous rock formations in Yosemite Valley include the Cathedral Rocks and the Cathedral Spires, which form the eastern side of the canyon in the valley; the Three Brothers, which consist of Eagle Peak,

Middle Brother, and Lower Brother; Sentinel Rock, opposite Yosemite Falls; and Glacier Point, an observation point some 3,214 feet (979 m) above the valley floor.

The naturalist John Muir spent a great deal of time in Yosemite and clearly held it in the highest regard. Writing for *Century Magazine* in 1890, Muir had this to say about Yosemite Valley:

> The walls of the valley are made up of rocks, mountains in size, partly separated from each other by side cañons and gorges; and they are so sheer in front, and so compactly and harmoniously built together on a level floor, that the place, comprehensively seen, looks like some immense hall or temple lighted from above. But no temple made with hands can compare with Yosemite.
>
> Every rock in its walls seems to glow with life. Some lean back in majestic repose; others, absolutely sheer or nearly so for thousands of feet, advance beyond their companions in thoughtful attitudes giving welcome to storms and calms alike, seemingly conscious, yet heedless of everything going on about them.

ABOUT GRANITE

The granite that Muir wrote about so eloquently was *intrusive igneous rock*, or rock that forms when *magma* (molten rock) cools and hardens underground. Geologists have further categorized intrusive igneous rock as either *plutonic* (so named for Pluto, mythical god of the underworld) or *hypabyssal*. Plutonic rocks typically make up massive rock formations that occur in mountainous areas, and hypabyssal rocks form smaller masses, which often occur in strips or sheets.

Granite is plutonic rock that cools slowly and crystallizes five to 10 miles (8 to 16 km) below the Earth's surface. It is coarse-grained and is a composite of hundreds of smaller bits of rock that cooled together below the surface of the Earth for long periods. Granite formations, which are a combination of the minerals quartz, feldspar, and mica, can be exposed at the surface when older rock above has eroded or ruptured and made way for the rock below. Because of its massive length, the Sierra Nevada is classified as a *batholith*, an immense mass of rock that comprises the core of many mountain ranges. The word *batholith* comes from a Greek word that means "deep rock."

Even after the granite has fully emerged, the rock continues to expand each time water freezes inside of it. The freeze-thaw process over the years causes the outer layers of granite to flake and peel from the surface in a process known as *exfoliation*, a form of weathering. As shown in the illustration on page 35, exfoliation produces rounded masses of rock.

© Infobase Publishing

This drawing of a boulder sliced in half shows how exfoliation affects granite.

Some 12 different types of granite have been identified in Yosemite National Park, and one large boulder abandoned by a glacier in the Merced River is said to be of yet another type. The differences in the granites are most often subtle and are revealed by differing responses to erosion. Granite with a high proportion of *silica*, compounds of metal with silicon and oxygen, is stronger and resists weathering better than other granite, which has a tendency to crack.

El Capitan is formed of the toughest granite in the world, which explains why glaciers failed to break it down. In honor of the stalwart cliff, this type of rock is now known as El Capitan granite. Though much of El Capitan is made up of the granite named for it, the world-famous cliff also contains additional types of granite. Geologists say El Capitan granite was the first of the granites in Yosemite Valley to form, over 100 million years ago.

THE SIERRA NEVADA

The Sierra Nevada, home to Yosemite National Park, lies primarily in eastern California, spreading just over the northwestern border of Nevada. The range stretches about 400 miles (640 km) long and from about 40 to 80 miles (60 to 130 km) wide, extending northwest from Tehachapi Pass near Bakersfield, California, to south of Lassen Peak, a cratered volcano not far from the city of Redding. The mountain range's altitude ranges from near sea level along the western edge to more than 13,000 feet (3,962 m) along the crest near Yosemite National Park and more than 14,000 feet (4,267 m) along the crest near Sequoia National Park and Kings Canyon National Park. Mount Whitney, which rises to 14,495 feet (4,418 m) in Sequoia National Park, is the highest peak not only in the Sierra Nevada but also in the continental United States.

In addition to granite, the Sierra Nevada also contains layered metamorphic rocks, remnants of ancient sedimentary and volcanic rocks that were altered by the intrusive igneous rock. Other remnants of metamorphic rocks remain from the original mountains that eroded or ruptured to make way for the granite. Geologists estimate that metamorphic rock comprises less than 5 percent of Yosemite National Park.

During the Paleozoic and Mesozoic eras (dating from 540 to 65 million years ago), a vast sea covered the area where the Sierra Nevada now stands. Ancient mountains that surrounded the sea routinely contributed sand, silt, and mud to the seafloor. Layers of this sediment eventually built up as layers of rock. Movement in the Earth's crust lifted these rock layers above sea level, tilting and positioning them to form a mountain range. By the end of the Cretaceous Period, about 65 million years ago, all that tilting and lifting caused the crest of the mountains to rupture and exposed the granite below. Today geologists rank the Sierra Nevada as the largest *tilted fault-block* range in the United States.

This slow process of uplifting and tilting—which still goes on today—gave the steep slopes of the Sierra Nevada their *grade*, or slope. About 25 million years ago, the Earth pushed the mountains still higher, which led to the steep *escarpment*, or cliffs, that characterize the eastern slopes of the range today. Streams that once had flowed gently through the area became more forceful, eroding the land into a sharper mountainous terrain and forming canyons as deep as 2,000 feet (609 m). Some 10 million years ago, the canyons were inundated and buried by volcanic lava flows and mudflows, and the streams cut deeper and deeper canyons into the range.

The Sierra Nevada reached its full height just about the time the ice age reached the area. Unable to melt due to the cold temperatures, snow collected over the years on top of layers of frozen ice. When the snow rose 100 feet (30 m) or higher, the ice underneath reacted to the pressure by pushing downward and slipping out from underneath the snow. These rivers of ice, or glaciers, slowly made their way through the mountain valleys previously carved by rivers and streams.

SHRINKING GLACIERS

A few small glaciers still exist today in the High Sierras, including one on Mount Lyell. The highest point in Yosemite National Park, Mount Lyell stands 13,114 feet (3,997 m) high. A survey conducted in 2003 revealed that the few glaciers that remain in the range appear to be shrinking dramatically. In some cases, the glaciers are disappearing completely.

Seven of the Sierra Nevada's glaciers are smaller than they were 100 years ago, according to Hassan Basagic, the graduate student at Portland State University who initiated the 2003 survey. Basagic's report concluded that, by 2005, the Lyell Glacier's protected west arm had diminished 30 percent since 1883, whereas its more exposed east arm had shrunk by 70 percent. Researchers suggest that the transformation of the Lyell Glacier and others is accelerating due to global warming.

YOSEMITE NATIONAL PARK

Yosemite National Park is about 1,170 square miles (3,030 km²), an area about the size of Rhode Island. The park includes 263 miles (423 km) of roads and 800 miles (1,287 km) of hiking trails. Elevations inside the park range from 2,000 feet (609 m) above sea level to more than 13,000 feet (3,962 m). Justifiably world famous for its breathtaking views, Yosemite Valley may be the most popular site, but it is a mere 5 percent of Yosemite National Park. The remaining 95 percent of the park is officially

---

DONNER PASS

Donner Pass is the most famous pass through the Sierra Nevada. Sometimes called a notch, a mountain pass is a geological feature lower than the surrounding peaks. At an elevation of 7,089 feet (2,161 m), Donner Pass is situated in the northern Sierra Nevada, close to Lake Tahoe, which is on the border between California and Nevada.

During the gold rush in the middle and late 1800s, thousands of fortune seekers and others hoping to settle out west went through Donner Pass to reach California. In the winter of 1846–47, a group of families from Illinois and Iowa made the trip, traveling as the Donner Party. The group, which numbered 87, took the name out of regard for two branches of the Donner family traveling with them.

After leaving Fort Bridger (in present-day Wyoming), where wagon trains typically stopped to replenish supplies, the Donner Party chose to take a little-used route west and encountered numerous delays. Party members argued frequently over the delays, and tensions ran high. After crossing the salt flats west of Great Salt Lake, they reached a lake in the Sierra Nevada. When the group camped at the lake and on a nearby creek, an early snowstorm blew through, trapping them. The bad weather continued, and the group's food supplies began to run low.

In December, part of the starving group opted to press on, to try to make it through the snow-choked passes. They failed, and many in the party died. The surviving members of the Donner Party may have turned to cannibalism to survive. Rescue expeditions from the Sacramento Valley were finally able to reach the remaining members of the group. About half of the original party eventually managed to reach California, but once there family loyalties were deeply divided regarding who caused the original delays that led to the disaster, now considered one of the most famous tragedies in the history of the American West.

Today Donner Lake is a popular mountain resort, named for the travelers. A monument is nearby, and Donner Pass, also named for the group, houses a weather observatory.

designated as wilderness, as decreed by Congress in 1984. The 1964 Wilderness Act declares that wilderness is "in contrast with those areas where man and his own works dominate the landscape, as an area where the earth and its community of life are untrammeled by man, where man himself is a visitor who does not remain."

Federal protection of Yosemite Valley came first. In response to pleas in 1864 from conservationists Frederick Law Olmsted and I. W. Raymond, President Abraham Lincoln signed a bill granting Yosemite Valley and the Mariposa Grove of Giant Sequoias—one of three groves of giant sequoias in the area—to the state of California. One tree believed to be 1,800 years old, known as the Grizzly Giant, stands in Mariposa Grove. These areas were to be "held for public use, resort and recreation" for all time. This grant was the first federal authorization to preserve scenic and scientific values for public benefit, and it served as a precursor for the concept of the state and national park systems.

On October 1, 1890, after naturalist John Muir protested devastation of meadows in the High Sierra, Yosemite National Park was established by an act of Congress. For a time, the U.S. military administered the park while the state governed the area originally set aside by Lincoln. In 1906, California turned over Yosemite Valley and the Mariposa Grove to the federal government. Ten years later, Congress established the National Park Service.

AN ABUNDANCE OF WATERFALLS

Yosemite National Park contains numerous waterfalls, and many of them are in Yosemite Valley. Perhaps the best known, after Yosemite Falls, is Bridalveil Fall, the first waterfall visible just beyond the western entrance of Yosemite National Park. Bridalveil Fall drops 620 feet (189 m) from the top of a granite cliff. Like Yosemite Falls, Bridalveil is a hanging valley waterfall that originates from a stream that runs along a rolling plateau behind the cliff. The waterfall is fed by melting snow.

Though Bridalveil Fall's watershed is smaller than that of Yosemite Creek, which feeds Yosemite Falls, the fall flows all year and also maintains a full flow later into the summer. Unlike that of Yosemite Falls, Bridalveil's watershed faces north, which results in less evaporation throughout the year. The meadow and forest behind Bridalveil Fall also provide a larger water storage capacity than the mostly barren granite above Yosemite Falls.

Vernal Fall, which can be viewed from Glacier Point, is also well known. Vernal Fall drops 317 feet (97 m) and flows all year, though when the flow decreases in late summer, the fall separates into two or three separate streams. Ribbon Fall, just west of El Capitan, is much taller than the better-known Vernal Fall. Ribbon Fall drops a dramatic 1,612 feet

Bridalveil Fall, a hanging valley waterfall, flows all year just beyond the western entrance of Yosemite National Park. *(Patricia Corrigan)*

(491 m) but flows only during the spring. Horsetail Fall, so named because it swishes from side to side in the wind from winter through early spring, drops 1,000 feet (305 m) just east of El Capitan. In mid-February, the orange glow of the sunset causes Horsetail Fall to appear to be on fire.

Additional waterfalls at Yosemite National Park include Silver Strand Fall, a towering 1,170 feet (357 m) high; Staircase Falls, which in spring flows 1,300 feet (396 m) down rocky ledges near Glacier Point; and Nevada Fall, which flows above Vernal Fall all year, with a drop of 594 feet (181 m).

EARLY RESIDENTS

Long before the National Park Service, John Muir, and Abraham Lincoln, Native Americans lived in what is now known as Yosemite National Park. History records that people lived in the area as early as 4,000 years ago. By the late 18th century, the Southern and Central Miwok tribes were well established in the area.

The Southern Miwok people called Yosemite Valley *awahni*, which means "Place like a gaping mouth." The word *Yosemite* is said to have originated from *yohemite*, the term used by Miwok living west of Yosemite to refer to the natives in the area that now is the park. The word *yohemite* translates as "Some of them are killers." During the 19th century, Native Americans from four other tribes joined the indigenous Miwok. Together they created a complex culture.

In 1833, Joseph Rutherford Walker and a group of accompanying explorers were said to be the first white men to see Yosemite Valley, though the party did not enter the area. After gold was discovered in the foothills of the Sierra Nevada in 1849, thousands of miners arrived, and hundreds of Miwok people were killed as a result. In 1851, the Mariposa Battalion, a state-sponsored militia, moved into Yosemite Valley in response to increasing conflicts. The government attempted to relocate the Miwok to a reservation on the Fresno River, but the effort failed. Whites and Europeans continued to settle in and around Yosemite Valley, changing forever the lives of the Native Americans.

The Yosemite Museum in Yosemite Valley displays artifacts that interpret the cultural history of Yosemite's native people from 1850 to the present. Behind the building, there is a reconstructed Indian village with several structures, including a sweat lodge and a roundhouse still used for spiritual ceremonies by descendants of the early Miwok. Graves of some Native Americans are among those in the Yosemite Cemetery.

FLORA AND FAUNA

Yosemite National Park is home to 1,400 species of flowering plants. A vast array of wildflowers typically start blooming in May at the lower elevations and make their presence known at the higher elevations in June or July. Among the types of wildflowers are buttercups, coneflowers, lemon bottlebrush, milkweed, shooting stars, violets, whorled penstemon, and wild ginger.

More than 35 different types of trees can be found in the park. Tree species include alder, aspen, black oak, canyon oak, cottonwood, Douglas

fir, incense cedar, lodgepole pine, maple, mountain hemlock, Pacific dog-
wood, red fir, redwood, sugar pine, white fir, and willow.

Some 80 species of mammals live in Yosemite National Park. Bears
occasionally are seen in the forests or in meadows along roads and trails.
Other mammals include badgers, bighorn sheep, bobcats, chipmunks,
coyotes, deer, mountain lions, raccoons, red foxes, and squirrels.

Birds, most often sighted in meadows, along rivers, or in forests, are
plentiful in the park. Nearly 240 species of birds have been sighted, including bald eagles, corn woodpeckers, great gray owls, mountain chicka-
dees, peregrine falcons, Steller's jays, and willow flycatchers.

ECOLOGICAL CHALLENGES

Automobiles were first permitted in Yosemite National Park in 1913.
In 1954, more than 1 million people visited the park, and that number
doubled by 1976. To offset the impact of such large crowds, park officials
declared many one-way roads and eliminated cars altogether in the east
end of Yosemite Valley. In 2003, almost 3.5 million people visited Yosemite National Park, most of them coming by car.

Over the years, free shuttle buses and trams were put into service
in the valley and in Mariposa Grove to take visitors around the park. In
the spring of 2005, a new fleet of 18 hybrid diesel/electric buses was
launched. Riders may disembark at a specific stop or stay on board to see
what lies ahead. Park officials report that the new buses have decreased
the noise level in the park by as much as 70 percent, and they anticipate
a reduction of 20 to 55 percent in fuel consumption.

One criticism leveled repeatedly at park management is that parts of
Yosemite Valley suffer from overcrowding. Others complain about the
shops and galleries, which seem to compete with the natural beauty of
the place. Officials have made one popular decision. When a severe flood
in 1997 destroyed half the campsites and one-third of the buildings, the
decision was made to allow the ravaged land to return to nature, rather
than to replace the damaged buildings.

IN THE FIELD: ROCKFALLS

In 2004, Gerald F. Wieczorek and James B. Snyder conducted a study
for the U.S. Geological Survey titled "Historical Rock Falls in Yosemite
National Park, California." The study produced an inventory of historical
rockfalls reported in Yosemite National Park between 1857 and 2004.
Data on 519 rockfalls included the location, date, type of slope movement, trigger, size or volume, type of damage, narrative description, and
references for the report on the fall.

The authors reported that 330 of the 519 rockfalls occurred in Yosemite Valley, and most others occurred nearby. Between 1857 and 2003,

rockfalls in Yosemite Valley killed 12 people and injured 62. Considering that more than 3 million people visit the national park each year, the number killed or injured is remarkably low.

The authors noted that although additional rockfalls had taken place, many had not been reported, either because of the small size of events or "the lack of impact on trails, roads, structures or utilities." In the report, *rockfall* was used as a collective term for rock falls, rock slides, debris slides, debris flows, debris slumps, and earth slumps.

The report reveals that causes of rockfalls have included rainstorms and earthquakes as well as periods of rapid snowmelt, wind, and "extreme freeze-thaw conditions." Other causes include slow infiltration of rainfall, exfoliation of slopes, weathering of rock, and root penetration. The authors noted that smaller rockfalls may follow large rockfalls, sometimes for days, weeks, or even months. After two large rockfalls from the granite cliff known as Middle Brother occurred, small rockfalls continued at the site for at least a month. Descriptions for all rockfalls included in the study were compiled from published and unpublished reports.

IN THE FIELD: WILDERNESS INTERRUPTED

One exception to the wilderness in Yosemite National Park is Hetch Hetchy, a valley that houses an eight-mile (12.5-km)-long reservoir on the Tuolumne River near the western boundary of the park. That reservoir, created by the O'Shaughnessy Dam, provides water and generates hydroelectric power to 2.4 million people in and around San Francisco. In a bow to the natural beauty of the area, the power-generation facilities and transmission lines are all concealed.

Opponents of the reservoir—and there are many—continue to advocate for relocation of the reservoir and restoration of Hetch Hetchy Valley as a wilderness site. The Sierra Club appointed a Hetch Hetchy Restoration Task Force. In 2004, Larry Fahn, then president of the organization, called for a full analysis of the feasibility and benefits of restoring Hetch Hetchy Valley. Results of the study were due late in 2006.

Fahn noted that the organization's restoration plan proposes collecting and storing the water downslope from Yosemite National Park in the High Sierras. Fahn called the proposed restoration "a fitting tribute to John Muir." The dam at the reservoir, which measures 430 feet (131 m) high, was first proposed in 1903. As president and founder of the Sierra Club, John Muir and his organization protested mightily.

Muir wrote, "Dam Hetch Hetchy! As well dam for water tanks the people's cathedrals and churches, for no holier temple has ever been consecrated by the heart of man." In spite of Muir's passionate disapproval, a bill was passed in 1913 to build the dam. Ten years later, it was in place. Since then controversy over the dam has erupted repeatedly. In 1987,

Don Hodel, then secretary of the Department of the Interior, requested a study of the effect of tearing down the O'Shaughnessy Dam. The report, prepared by the National Park Service, concluded that if the reservoir were drained, a forest would grow on the land within 50 years.

Officers of the Sierra Club immediately claimed that the true purpose of the study was to divide the environmental movement by forcing residents of San Francisco—who understandably want to maintain the source of their water and electricity—to come out against an environmental issue. Regardless of any perceived ulterior motive on the part of the Department of the Interior, today the people of San Francisco continue to resist draining the reservoir.

THE LEGACY OF YOSEMITE

Attention paid to Yosemite Falls over the years has been fitting tribute to the highest freefalling waterfall in North America and the fifth tallest in the world. Presidents and poets have visited Yosemite Falls. Famous photographers—Ansel Adams and Galen Rowell among them—have captured the falls in breathtaking photographs.

Through the years, perhaps no one has written more eloquently about Yosemite Falls than John Muir. "This noble fall has by far the richest, as well as the most powerful voice of all the falls of the Valley," he wrote. The falls, as well as the rest of Yosemite National Park, led Muir to pen this tribute: "As long as I live, I'll hear waterfalls and birds and winds sing. I'll interpret the rocks, learn the language of flood, storm, and the avalanche. I'll acquaint myself with the glaciers and wild gardens, and get as near the heart of the world as I can."

Gavarnie Falls
Western Europe

The Grande Cascade de Gavarnie, also known as Gavarnie Falls, is surrounded by a dozen or more waterfalls, but even in the presence of other falls—known locally as mountain torrents, or, in French, *gaves*—Gavarnie Falls stands out. The tallest waterfall in western Europe, Gavarnie Falls is in the Cirque de Gavarnie, a large glacial amphitheater in the central Pyrenees Mountains that stretch along the border between southeastern France and northwestern Spain.

Situated in Pyrenees National Park, Gavarnie Falls drops 1,400 feet (425 m) from a high cliff face. A rock ledge juts out near the bottom, briefly interrupting the flow of the fall. The highest single drop measures 922 feet (281 m). The average width of the fall is only 50 feet (15 m). Gavarnie Falls is said to produce an average volume of 1,496 gallons (5,662 L) per second. Present all year, Gavarnie Falls reaches its maximum volume in summer, when melting snow from the Pyrenees Mountains feeds the waterfall. Like Yosemite Falls in Yosemite National Park, Gavarnie Falls impresses because of its height, rather than width or volume, and because of the natural beauty of its setting, shown in the lower color insert on page C-3.

THE CIRQUE

The Cirque de Gavarnie is a semicircle of mountainous cliffs at the upper end of a valley. A *cirque* is a steep-sided circular hollow, a landform that is created when a *glacier*, or river of ice, causes a mountain to erode. The pressure from the retreating compacted snow and ice forms a natural bowl-shaped amphitheater at the head of a U-shaped trough, as shown in the illustration on page 45. The Cirque de Gavarnie is believed to be 20,000 years old. The massive amphitheater measures nearly 5,500 feet (1,676 m) high and 2,625 feet (800 m) in diameter. The circumference of the base of the cirque measures more than two miles (3 km), and, at its highest point, the cirque measures nearly nine miles (14 km). To put that in perspective, the cirque is large enough to accommodate 15 million visitors at once.

The beauty of the spot has long been recognized. Victor Hugo (1802–85), the prolific French novelist and poet best known for *The Hunchback of Notre Dame* and *Les Misérables*, described Cirque de Gavarnie

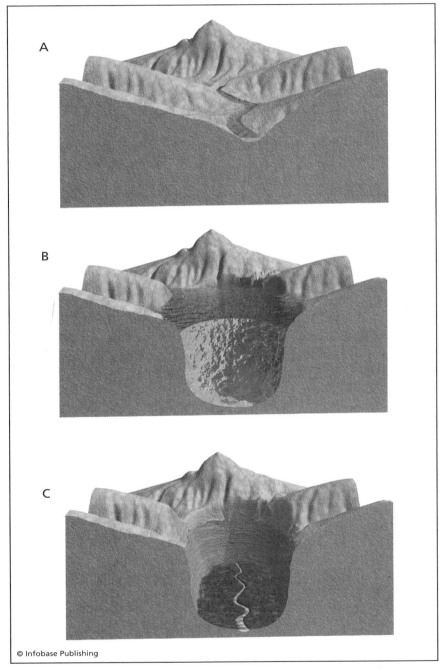

This illustration shows how glaciers and ice sheets gouge out cirques and gorges.

ICE CAVES OF GAVARNIE

In 1926, Norbert Casteret—later known as the father of modern cave exploring—discovered several ice caves in the Pyrenees, some of the highest-known ice caves in the world. Ice caves, like the one shown in the photo below, often contain subterranean glaciers, rivers of ice with their own frozen waterfalls that exist deep inside mountains. Casteret (1897–1987) called these rivers "among the most strange and most rare phenomenon on this planet."

Ice caves can house subterranean glaciers, rivers of ice deep inside mountains. *(National Oceanic and Atmospheric Administration/Department of Commerce)*

As recorded in Casteret's book *The Darkness under the Earth,* he set out from the town of Gavarnie with his wife, Elizabeth, his brother, and his mother to explore Mount Perdu and search for caves. They encountered a snowstorm on the way and spent one night on the Spanish side of the Pyrenees in a small cave known as Villa Gaurier, named for the glaciologist who discovered it in 1906.

The next day, Casteret discovered a porch, the outer edge of an ice cave, some 98 feet (30 m) wide that led to a cave containing a frozen lake. "I looked in, and immediately I was in the grip of the demon Adventure, the fascination

as "nature's coliseum" and noted that the landform was "the most mysterious creation by the most mysterious of architects." Tourists who wish to see the Cirque de Gavarnie must travel the same way Hugo did—on foot, by donkey, or by horse from Gavarnie, a tourist town of fewer than 100 people. In medieval times, the town was a resting place for pilgrims traveling to Santiago de Compostela, a Christian shrine in northwestern Spain. Situated at an elevation of 4,452 feet (1,357 m), Gavarnie was home to some of the first mountain guides in the Pyrenees in the 19th century. The 2.5-mile (4-km) trip from the town to the waterfall takes about an hour.

Three mountains stand just behind the Cirque de Gavarnie, each rising about 9,800 feet (2,987 m). Jagged peaks of two others are to the east. At the center is a rocky ridge. Nearby is the Brèche-de-Roland, a vertical *gap*, or breach, in the rock, some 328 feet (100 m) deep and 196 of the unknown," wrote Casteret. The group opted to continue on to Mount Perdu, but Casteret and his wife returned one month later to investigate the cave. Upon hearing of the discovery, the French Alpine Club named the ice cave the Grotte Glacee Casteret, which is still recognized as the highest ice cave in the area.

In 1950, Casteret and two of his five children (daughters Maud and Gilberte) discovered five additional ice caves on the Spanish side of the Cirque de Gavarnie. In *The Darkness under the Earth*, Casteret writes of climbing down rope ladders with his daughters to stand on clear, frozen rivers of ice with sediment visible some 10 feet (3 m) below. He recalls that they came upon a gallery of transparent, octagonal ice crystals, some of them eight to 10 inches (20 to 25 cm) in diameter. "It was an incredible sight," he writes. "We stood inside a geode of a sparkling ice, a veritable crystal palace, a thing impossible to describe." He also tells of bumping his head on a crystal-clear stalactite.

Born August 19, 1897, in the village of Saint-Martory at the base of the French Pyrenees, Casteret first visited a cave at the age of five. He claimed that on that day he became fascinated with the "eternal darkness" found in caves. Though he made his living as a notary public, Casteret never lost his interest in *speleology*, the study of caving. He spent much of his life exploring caves, unearthing prehistoric sculptures, and discovering prehistoric cave art. Casteret wrote 43 books about his adventures, many of which were translated into other languages.

In the foreword to Casteret's first book, *Ten Years under the Earth*, published in 1933, Édouard-Alfred Martel—the man credited with founding the science of speleology—wrote this: "Three precious qualities make Casteret's work significant and successful: the daring (sometimes too great) with which he attacks obstacles that have stopped his predecessors (especially the dangerous 'siphons' or submerged tunnels); the order and method with which he plans his work and perseveres in a subject once begun; and finally the self discipline which enables him to learn from and lean upon those who can teach him."

Casteret served in World War I and was an avid sportsman all his life. He prided himself on staying physically fit. He enjoyed soccer, diving, skiing, rowing, pole vaulting, and other sports. Still, caving was his favorite way to spend time. "Speleology is sport in commission of science," Casteret said on more than one occasion. Casteret died in Toulouse on July 20, 1987. In 2000, the French government honored him by issuing a postage stamp featuring his photo.

feet (60 m) wide. Legend has it that Roland de Roncevaux, a nephew of Charlemagne and a soldier in the French court in the 770s, slashed through the mountain with his sword, known as Durendal. Other snow-capped peaks are nearby.

Additional natural amphitheaters in the area are the Cirque de Troumouse and the Cirque d'Estaubé. Troumouse, which is more isolated and desolate than Gavarnie, is the larger of the two, some six miles (10 km) long and with cliffs 3,280 feet (1,000 m) high. Estaubé sits between Gavarnie and Troumouse and is difficult to reach.

THE PYRENEES

The Cirque de Gavarnie shares the geologic history of the Pyrenees Mountains, which extend in an almost straight line some 270 miles (435 km) from the Bay of Biscay on the Atlantic Ocean to Cap de Creus on the Mediterranean Sea. The central section of the Pyrenees—home to the Cirque de Gavarnie—is the highest. Peaks there include Pico de Aneto in Spain, which is 11,168 feet (3,404 m) high, and Pic de Vignemale in France, which tops out at 10,820 feet (3,297 m). Other peaks of note include Monte Perdido in Spain and Pic du Midi d'Ossau in France. Peaks in the Pyrenees that extend above 6,000 feet (1,830 m) are snowcapped yearlong.

Geologists say the Pyrenees are older than the Alps. The sediments that led to the formation of the mountains were deposited during the Paleozoic and Mesozoic eras (from 65 to 230 million years ago), primarily in coastal basins. The Gulf of Gascony (today known as the Bay of Biscay) fanned out in the Lower Cretaceous period some 65 million years ago, which shoved what was the island of Iberia (modern-day Spain and Portugal) into France, capturing large layers of sediment. The pressure from the gulf and the movement in the Earth's crust combined to form the chain of mountains, which were in place by the time of the Eocene Epoch, some 38 to 53 million years ago.

The maximum width of the mountains is about 80 miles (130 km). Spain claims about two-thirds of the range, which covers some 21,380 square miles (55,373 km²). Walking the entire length of the range is a popular sport, much like walking the Appalachian Trail in the United States. Frederic Parrot, a French citizen, is said to be the first person to have walked the length of the Pyrenees. His trek took place in 1817 and lasted 53 days.

The principality of Andorra—belonging to neither France nor Spain— sits amid the peaks of the Pyrenees. The small principality covers about 468 square miles (1,212 km²), which is about two-and-a-half times the size of Washington, D.C. Some 70,500 people live in Andorra, where the tallest peak is 9,965 feet (2,946 m) high. Portions of six French departments (counties) and six Spanish provinces are also located in the Pyrenees Mountains. The border between Spain and France was established with the signing of the Peace of the Pyrenees in 1659.

GEOLOGIC MAKEUP

The eastern part of the Pyrenees, which formed first, boasts primarily granite and *gneiss*, a metamorphic rock that is similar to granite but contains banding, or streaking, showing sedimentary origins. Some streaks in the gneiss (pronounced "niece") may be the result of the remelting of magma, which is igneous rock, but most gneiss is metamorphic rock, formed from sand and clay.

Granite forms when molten rock cools and hardens underground, crystallizing five to 10 miles (8 to 16 km) below the Earth's surface. Granite, resistant to erosion and known for its strength, gets credit for the unworn character of the Pyrenees Mountains.

In the western part of the Pyrenees, layers of *limestone* lie against the base of granite peaks. Limestone, a *sedimentary* rock, is typically 50 percent calcium carbonate, which is formed primarily from accumulated skeletons of organisms, including shells and coral that once lay at the bottom of shallow seas.

In general, metallic ores in the Pyrenees Mountains are of little significance, though two areas have small iron mines. The Spanish slopes contain coal deposits that could be of economic value, but the French side has numerous beds of *lignite*, the lowest grade of coal. Lignite has only about 65 percent carbon compared to *anthracite* coal, which is almost pure carbon. Full of moisture, lignite produces the least amount of heat and the most smoke of any coal. Lead, manganese, and zinc are also found in the Pyrenees, and marble and slate quarries are also in the area.

Mineral springs are plentiful in the Pyrenees Mountains. In the valley of the Gave de Pau, Cauterets, Saint-Sauveur, and Barèges are the three most popular hot springs, each rich in sulfur and sodium. In the valley of the Adour Bagnres, hot and cold springs occur that contain calcium sulfates, iron, sulfur, and sodium. Near Lannemezan, Capvern Springs contains calcium sulfates. Hot springs occur where warm or hot groundwater bubbles up on a regular basis. Typically, the water is significantly above the temperature at ground level. Hot springs are full of minerals, and people seek them out to bathe and relax in the water.

MOUNTAIN STREAMS

Three principal streams run through Hautes-Pyrénées: the Gave de Pau, the Neste, and the Adour. The water from Gavarnie Falls serves as the head of the Gave de Pau, a river made up of several mountain streams. The Gave de Pau flows through several valleys to just south of Lourdes. From there, Gave de Pau turns northwest to join the Adour River, where the two travel on as Les Gaves Réunis.

The headwaters of the Neste, a tributary of the Garonne, are also in the Cirque de Gavarnie and on the slopes of nearby Cirque de Troumouse. The Adour River descends from the Pic du Midi, flows through the valley of Campan, and leaves the mountains. The river then divides into numerous channels and irrigates the plain of Tarbes, the city closest to Cirque de Gavarnie.

The largest channel, the Canal d'Alaric, stretches some 22 miles (36 km). Beyond Hautes-Pyrénées, the Arros River joins the Canal d'Alaric, and together the rivers run through the department from south to north-northwest. Eventually, the Gave de Pau joins the Arros. Streams from the Pic de Vignemale come together at the towns of Luz and Pierrefitte. Because the Gave de Pau is considered a mountain stream, it is regarded as a tributary of the Adour after leaving Lourdes.

PIC DU MIDI OBSERVATORY

Gavarnie Falls at the Cirque de Gavarnie is not the only world-famous attraction in the Hautes-Pyrénées. The Pic du Midi Observatory, known for achievements in astronomy, is perched on an isolated summit at an altitude of 9,470 feet (2,890 m), just nine miles (15 km) south of the Cirque de Gavarnie.

Over the years, scientists working at the Pic du Midi Observatory have mapped planetary surfaces, determined the period of rotation of Venus, and calculated preparations for the Apollo landings on the Moon. Other fields of research conducted at the observatory include earth magnetism, atmospheric physics, seismology, natural radioactivity, glaciology, cosmic-ray physics, and botany.

The Pic du Midi Observatory, once a weather station, sits high on an isolated peak in the Pyrenees Mountains that stretch between France and Spain. *(James Silvester)*

Shown in the photograph at left, the Pic du Midi Observatory houses a Bernard Lyot telescope (the largest in France), a Nicmos infrared camera, and a smaller telescope mainly used for planetary research. The site is considered one of the best in the world for solar observations.

Since 2000, the observatory has been open to the public. The building complex includes a museum, a restaurant, and observation terraces. The breathtaking view allows visitors a look at almost the entire Pyrenees mountain range from the Basque Country to Andorra. On clear nights, the lights from the resort town of Biarritz, some 93 miles (149 km) away, are visible, and halos of light can be seen in Barcelona, some 150 miles (241 km) away.

The vision of two men led to the construction of the Pic du Midi Observatory. Charles Champion du Bois de Nansouty, a retired army general, and Célestin-Xavier Vaussenat, a construction engineer, developed a temporary meteorological station in 1873. They then raised the money to build a more permanent weather station. When the observatory was opened in August 1882, the founders offered to donate it to the state in return for yearly allowances to maintain their salaries as directors. The offer was accepted, and the weather station became a national observatory supervised by the Central Bureau of Meteorology in Paris.

Employees at the observatory originally had to walk to work, a five-to-eight-hour trek. In the summer, mules carried coal, potatoes, wine, wood, drinking water, and other supplies to the summit. Porters brought food up the rest of the year, weather permitting. In 1949, an elevating platform was constructed to transport staff and supplies to the peak. In 1952, a cable-car system was built to carry visiting scientists to the top. The trip today, in a modernized version of the cable car, takes just 15 minutes from La Mongie, a resort 25 miles (41 km) from the village of Gavarnie.

Once the Neste d'Aure descends from the peaks of Nouvielle and Troumouse, the stream joins the Neste de Louron at Arreau and flows northward through a valley, continuing as far as La Barthe. There the river turns east and furnishes the plateau of Lannemezan with a canal (the Canal de la Neste). Residents use the water for irrigation and to supply small streams in the area that dry up every summer.

CLIMATE

Gavarnie Falls is in the Midi-Pyrénées, the largest region of France. Within this region is the department of Hautes-Pyrénées, similar to a county. Hautes-Pyrénées was founded in 1790, developed from a mixture of districts. The department stretches over 1,750 square miles (4,532 km^2). In the highlands of Hautes-Pyrénées, the climate in winter is quite cold, with severe weather and violent winds. The area receives more than 78 inches (198 cm) of precipitation each year, much of it as snow. In summer strong thunderstorms typically occur several times a week.

Even if passage between the mountains were possible in winter—a season that lasts six to seven months each year—the Pyrenees Mountains in this area have curiously few passes. Only two, both at higher elevations, are suitable for cars. The Southern Railway crosses from the west side of the mountains to the east by the main line from Bayonne to Toulouse.

Tarbes, the capital of Hautes-Pyrénées, is in the northern part of the department, about a 45-minute drive from the mountains. The average annual rainfall in town is about 34 inches (86 cm). In the northern range, rain falls far more often than in the south. On the nearby plains, the weather varies widely, with hot summers, mild autumns and winters, and rainy springs.

PYRENEES NATIONAL PARK

Gavarnie Falls is located in Pyrenees National Park. Established in 1967, the park covers 180 square miles (466 km^2), stretching some 60 miles (100 km) along the border between France and Spain. Hundreds of high-altitude lakes lie within the boundaries of the park. Only about 12 percent of the park is wooded. Springs and heavy snowfall feed the numerous streams and brooks that run through the forests. Some 215 miles (350 km) of trails wind through the park, some of which are linked with trails in Spain.

Economic development in the park and just beyond has been limited over the past 50 years to livestock grazing in the mountains and to tourism. Some 2 million tourists visit the park each year, where they hike, bicycle, climb, ski, and fish. Park officials are working to limit road construction and vehicle use.

Pyrenees National Park shares a tract of land nine miles (15 km) long with its Spanish counterpart, the Ordesa and Monte Perdido National Park. In 1997, the Franco-Spanish Gavarnie–Monte Perdido range was registered as a UNESCO World Heritage Site under the name "Pyrénées Monte Perdido Cirques et Canyons."

FLORA AND FAUNA

Three-quarters of the mammals native to France live in the Pyrenees. Mammals protected in the park include the brown bear, lynx, chamois, and marmot. The chamois and marmot both faced almost certain extinction elsewhere in France. Two species known to be extinct elsewhere live in the Pyrenees Mountains. One is the capercaillie, a game bird. The second is the desman, a small aquatic mole. The bear population has been in decline for some 30 years, and only a few individual bears remain in the park today. Endangered birds of prey sighted in Pyrenees National Park include the bearded vulture and golden eagle.

Flora in the park are also protected, from the dwarf willows at the alpine level above 7,874 feet (2,400 m) to the birch and fir trees at the lower levels. Radish-leaved bittercress, Pyrenean iris, and Pyrenean valerian are among the flowers in the park. About 160 plant species are *endemic*, or native, to the Pyrenees Mountains.

HAUTES-PYRÉNÉES

In contrast to the southern portion of Hautes-Pyrénées, which boasts the high peaks of the Central Pyrenees Mountains, the imposing cirques, and the dramatic waterfalls, the northern portion of the department consists of rolling plains and hills. Wheat and corn are the primary crops on the plains. Rye, oats, and barley flourish in the highlands. Vineyards stretch across Madiran and Peyrigure, an area where tobacco is also cultivated. Chestnut trees and fruit trees are planted on the lower slopes.

Tarbes, the capital, is horse country. Horses bred in the region are a fusion of Arab, English, and Navarrese bloodlines. Cattle, sheep, and goats are also raised throughout the area. Tarbes is also home to a large military arsenal. Industry in the department includes flourmills, sawmills, paper mills, tanneries, and factories where agricultural implements are made. Looms are also crafted in the area, which is known for the manufacture of knitted goods.

HUMAN HISTORY

Based on artifacts recovered from caves in the Ariège, Couserans, and Comminges regions of the Pyrenees, humans lived in the Pyrenees Mountains thousands of years before history recorded their presence. Today the Catalans live in the eastern end of the mountains, and the Basques inhabit the western end. Languages spoken along the range include Catalan, Aranese, Aragonese, and Euskera. Additional dialects are also present.

There was a time when each valley functioned as a mini-fiefdom, fending off the influence of central government—and of other independent-minded valleys—by virtue of isolation. During the Spanish Civil War and World War II, persons out of favor, politically speaking, paid shepherds and smugglers to hide them in the mountains. In more recent times, French men and women disillusioned with the government retreated into the isolated valleys. Even today people cross back and forth from France to Spain, disregarding official boundaries in favor of the sense of community shared by those who dwell among the Pyrenees Mountains.

IN THE FIELD: STREAM ECOLOGY

Since the early 1990s, scientists from the School of Geography, Earth and Environmental Sciences at the University of Birmingham, United Kingdom, have been conducting studies on the alpine streams in the Taillon-Gabiétous *catchment*, or drainage basin, adjacent to the Cirque de Gavarnie. One project, under the direction of Dr. Lee Brown, now at the University of Leeds, is designed to reveal through natural chemical tracers the sources of alpine streams fed by snow, glaciers, and groundwater.

By taking samples throughout the summer, researchers observe the changes in water sourcing. During late May and June, streams are sourced mainly from snowmelt originating in large snow packs that cover the upper mountain peaks. As these snow packs melt, they recharge groundwater stores in soils and rocks, and those groundwater stores begin to feed the streams. By late July, the snow packs have almost completely melted, exposing the glaciers at the higher altitudes, above 8,202 feet (2,500 m).

Each water source produces different volumes of water with distinct chemical signatures, while at the same time influencing other stream characteristics such as water temperature and concentrations of suspended sediment. Brown noted in an interview that "the snowmelt is relatively dilute and cold whereas in contrast, the groundwater is chemically enriched and relatively warm. Water draining from the glaciers is also relatively dilute and cold but has much higher concentrations of suspended sediment than snowmelt and groundwater streams."

The research team also seeks to understand how these stream characteristics influence insect larvae (stoneflies and mayflies, for example) that live in the streams. Any changes in the insect populations could have important implications for understanding the impacts of future changes in the biodiversity of the streams, because researchers expect that the relatively predictable summer water sources will be altered over time with climate change. Such changes may make the streams unsuitable for some species that currently live in these streams.

According to Brown, some of the insect populations near Gavarnie Falls are native to the French Pyrenees and not found in any other region of the world. In turn the insects also function as food for fish, reptiles, and birds, so the potential effects of changing water sourcing could be wide-ranging.

The Birmingham research group is at the forefront of understanding hydrological and climatological influences on water temperatures in alpine streams. Earlier studies by the group have included looking at algae, baseline surveys of stream invertebrates within other parts of the Cirque de Gavarnie, and detailed studies of how meteorological conditions influence the seasonal melting patterns of the Taillon Glacier.

MELTING GLACIERS

Greenpeace released a report late in 2004 stating that the glaciers on the Spanish side of the Pyrenees were melting fast. According to the report, the total surface area of the glaciers had dropped from 4,396 acres (1,779 ha) in 1894 to 716 acres (290 ha) in 2000, a drop of 85 percent. More than 50 percent of the melting has occurred in the last 20 years, with 30 percent occurring between 1991 and 2001.

Enrique Serrano from the Universidad de Valladolid and Eduardo Martínez de Pisón from the Autónoma de Madrid, both professors of geography, led the team of scientists that prepared the report for Greenpeace. In 1980, 27 glaciers still existed in the Pyrenees Mountains. In 2000, there were only 10. The scientists determined that the surface area of the glacier on Spain's towering Monte Perdido (10,941 feet [3,335 m] high) could deplete to only 22 acres (9 ha) by 2050. They predicted that the ice could disappear completely somewhere between 2050 and 2070.

The scientists attribute the dramatic change to human-induced climate change. Even opponents of that theory admit that humans may well be the cause of accelerated melting. Norbert Casteret, the Frenchman who discovered some of the highest ice caves in the world, took an optimistic view regarding global warming. In his book *The Darkness under the Earth*, he wrote: "I wonder how many thousand years will pass before a change of climate melts the ice, restores the flow of water, and enables it to recommence its work of burrowing deeper and deeper through the rock; and how many more thousand years will pass before the whole network of these caves dries out and becomes fossilized, so that one day speleologists will venture to follow the waterways yet deeper. …"

5

Niagara Falls

North America

The world-famous Niagara Falls, a series of three thundering waterfalls that graces the border of the United States and Canada, sets standards by which other falls are measured. The most voluminous waterfall in North America, the three-part falls that occurs on the Niagara River puts on an impressive show in a beautiful setting, drawing 14 million tourists from around the globe each year.

The individual waterfalls are the American Falls and Bridal Veil Falls in Niagara Falls, New York, and Horseshoe Falls, which is in Niagara Falls, Ontario, a province of Canada. People often refer to both the American Falls and Bridal Veil Falls collectively as simply the American Falls. A photo of both the American Falls and Horseshoe Falls is shown in the upper color insert on page C-4.

Horseshoe Falls, the largest of the three, measures 170 feet (52 m) high, and the crest extends about 2,500 feet (750 m). Horseshoe Falls takes its name from the gentle curve it makes from the Canadian riverbank to the edge of Goat Island, a piece of U.S. property in the middle of the Niagara River. Made of sediment from a now defunct glacial lake, Goat Island was named for a lone goat that survived a harsh winter there in the early 1770s.

The American Falls is 1,060 feet (320 m) wide and drops 190 feet (58 m). In 1954, a huge rockslide scattered boulders (known as *talus*) at the bottom of this fall, so the clear drop covers only about only 70 feet (21 m). Luna Island, a small chunk of land hovering at the southern edge of the American Falls, separates the flowing water into two parts. The narrower stream of water, known as Bridal Veil Falls, is about 40 feet (12 m) wide. Bridal Veil Falls has previously been known as Luna Falls and Iris Falls.

Horseshoe Falls carries about 90 percent of the river's water into the gorge below. Due to the immense force of the water, the plunge pool beneath Horseshoe Falls is over 100 feet (35 m) deep. Together the American Falls and Bridal Veil Falls send 75,750 gallons (286,714 L) of water

The full power of Horseshoe Falls is best experienced from a viewing platform directly adjacent to the thundering wall of water. *(Patricia Corrigan)*

over the brink every second, enough water to fill 7,556 10-gallon (37-L) fish tanks. The larger Horseshoe Falls boasts a volume of 681,750 gallons (2,580,424 L) per second—enough to flush more than 135,000 toilets or to fill 18,000 bathtubs.

The volume at Niagara Falls varies on all three falls from season to season, even from hour to hour, as giant *power plants*, massive buildings that convert water to electricity, located below the falls regulate the river's flow by drawing water above the falls into their reservoirs. The flow is greatest during the daytime in June, July, and August—peak tourist season. Even then, the flow is held to about half of what is possible were the river allowed to run free.

Niagara Falls is situated on the Niagara River, a *strait*, or channel, that runs between Lake Erie and Lake Ontario. The boundary line between the United States and Canada runs right down the middle of the Niagara

River. Legend has it that the word *Niagara* is derived from an Iroquois word that means "neck" or "split in the flatland."

THE COLOR OF WATER

At night all three sections of Niagara Falls are illuminated with pink, yellow, blue, and purple lights. During the day, Niagara Falls appears to be tinted a fresh shade of light green, but in this case, Mother Nature provides the color. The Niagara River is remarkably clear of sediment and sludge, which causes other rivers to run brown. The green tinge is a result of algae, air bubbles, dissolved salts, and finely ground rock (also known as *rock flour*) grabbed from the limestone riverbed and other rock along the way. Some 60 tons (54 metric tons) of dissolved minerals hurtle over Niagara Falls every minute.

In 1880, Frederick Law Olmsted proposed a design for Niagara Reservation State Park, now known as Niagara Falls State Park. (He also designed Central Park in New York City and Golden Gate Park in San Francisco.) Olmsted had this to say about the color of water at Niagara Falls: "As the river courses far below the Falls, confined between vast walls of rock, the clear water of a peculiar greenish hue, and white here and there with circlets of yet unsoothed foam, the effect is startlingly beautiful, quite apart from the Falls."

In 1842, author Charles Dickens visited Niagara Falls for the first time and commented: "It was not until I came to Table Rock [a viewing point on the Canadian side], and looked, Great Heaven, on what a fall of bright green water, that it came upon me in its full might and majesty." Just a few years earlier, in an article titled "Winter Studies and Summer Rambles in Canada" that was published in 1838, Anna Brownell Jameson recorded her impression of Niagara Falls: "As we approached the Table Rock, the whole scene assumed a wild and wonderful magnificence; down came the dark-green waters, hurrying with them over the edge of the precipice enormous blocks of ice brought down from Lake Erie."

HISTORY OF NIAGARA FALLS

Samuel de Champlain, a French explorer credited with founding the city of Quebec, was among the first European visitors at Niagara Falls. Champlain was in the area in 1604. A controversy exists to this day among some historians who debate whether Champlain visited the falls or simply wrote a description in his journal that was based on eyewitness accounts from members of his party.

In 1675, Louis Hennepin, a Franciscan missionary, went to Canada with French explorer René-Robert Cavelier, sieur de La Salle. The two traveled with a party that claimed all manner of land and water for France. Three years later, while La Salle was picking up supplies back in Kingston,

DAREDEVILS PAST AND PRESENT

In addition to tourists, Niagara Falls draws those who wish to conquer—or at least interact directly with—the rushing water. Sam Patch, who went by the more colorful name of the Yankee Leaper, jumped into the Niagara River from the cliff on Goat Island in 1829. Years later, he died after jumping from Genesee Falls in Rochester, New York. In 1901, schoolteacher Annie Taylor, then 63, went over Niagara Falls in a barrel. She was the first person known to survive the 170-foot (52-m) drop. Taylor lived to tell the tale, and afterward she set up a table at the falls where she charged people for a look at her barrel—until her manager stole it. Taylor died a pauper.

Since then more than a dozen people have intentionally gone over the falls in or on some type of container. Some survived. Some drowned. Others were badly injured. Such stunts are illegal, and the perpetrators are charged and must pay heavy fines—if they live.

Some daredevils have chosen to cross the river on tightropes. Jean François "Blondin" Gravelet was the first. In 1859, Gravelet stepped carefully across a high wire strung across the gorge just down river from Niagara Falls. In 1883, Matthew Webb tried to swim the rapids below the falls. Webb had had some experience with water—he was the first man to swim the English Channel—but he drowned in the Niagara River.

For all the wrong reasons, these daredevil acts brought crowds to Niagara Falls. Marilyn Monroe accomplished the same thing with much less risk, greatly increasing tourism in 1953 after starring in the movie *Niagara*. In 1980, the falls provided a cinematic backdrop for the movie *Superman II*. Later an IMAX movie was made about Niagara Falls. In early 2004, the falls was the location for the television series *Wonderfalls*. Film and TV stars aside, perhaps the most enduring tribute was the naming of asteroid #12382 *Niagara Falls*.

Today a new breed of daredevils is emerging. At the Grand Island Bridge two miles (3 km) from Niagara Falls—known as The Point of No Return—flashing lights and warning buoys alert boaters to go no farther on the Niagara River. Most boaters pay attention, but some do not. Those who do not—whether under the influence of alcohol or simply filled with reckless bravado—end up running their craft on the rocks at the edge of the river to avoid being swept over the falls. Local rescue units must then tow the boats to shore.

Visitors close to the thundering falls take risks as well. Signs on Luna Island, Goat Island, and Three Sisters Islands all warn against climbing on the slippery rocks at the edge of the water or stepping into the river for a quick photo. For various reasons, people ignore the signs. If they were to slip, the rushing water would carry them to the edge of the falls—and over—in 30 to 40 seconds. Usually, nothing happens, and these foolhardy tourists go on with the rest of their day. That said, park rangers report at least one or two accidents a week during tourist season, which runs from May through October.

Ontario, members of the Seneca tribe led Hennepin and others in the party to Niagara Falls. After returning to France in 1682, Hennepin wrote of his visit there, the first written record known to be based on an actual sighting. His book, *Nouvelle Decouverte* (New discovery), also included an engraving of Niagara Falls based on Hennepin's description. That engraving, by Dutch artist J. van Vienan, was not particularly accurate, but it is credited with sparking interest among Europeans about Niagara Falls.

"Betwixt the Lake Ontario and Erie there is a vast and prodigious column of water, which falls down after a surprising and astonishing manner, inasmuch as the Universe does not afford a parallel," Hennepin wrote. "'Tis true it and Swedenland boast of some such things; but we may well say that they are sorry patterns when compared to this of which we now speak. At the foot of this horrible precipice we meet the Niagara River which is not above one-quarter league broad, but is wonderfully deep in places. It is so rapid above the descent that it violently hurries down the wild beasts while endeavoring to pass it to feed on the other side, they not being able to withstand the force of its current, which invariably cast them headlong about 183 metres high."

Scholars took issue with Hennepin's mathematical estimates. Early in the 18th century, Finnish-Swedish naturalist Peter Kalm took part in an expedition to Niagara Falls. When he recorded his impressions, he also disputed Hennepin's account. In a letter to a friend in Philadelphia, written in 1750, Kalm said, "Hennepin has gained little credit in Canada; the name of honor they give him there is *un grand menteur* [a great liar]."

THE GREAT LAKES

Four of the Great Lakes—Superior, Michigan, Huron, and Erie—are the source for all the light-green water that pours over Niagara Falls. Lake Ontario, the fifth of the Great Lakes, accepts the water that drains from the other four and directs it to the St. Lawrence Seaway, which spills into the Atlantic Ocean at the Gulf of St. Lawrence. Considered individually, the lakes rank among the 14 largest bodies of freshwater.

Collectively, the Great Lakes have a total shoreline of about 10,000 miles (16,093 km), more than 350 species of fish, and provide drinking water for over 40 million people. The combined area of the Great Lakes is 94,250 square miles (244,160 km²), an area larger than the United Kingdom. The drainage basin of the lakes, which includes the lakes themselves and their connecting waterways, covers about 201,460 square miles (521,830 km²) extending nearly 690 miles (1,110 km) from north to south and about 860 miles (1,384 km) from Lake Superior in the west to Lake Ontario in the east.

If the Great Lakes were suddenly to spill every last drop, all of North America would be covered in about 3.5 feet (1 m) of water. That will not happen, of course. Nor will the Great Lakes dry up. They are constantly replenished by groundwater as well as rain, sleet, snow, and hail. Average annual rainfall in the Great Lakes is 36 inches (91 cm). The average annual evaporation rate in the Great Lakes is 24 inches (60 cm).

Lake Erie collects water draining from Lake Superior, Lake Michigan, Lake Huron, and assorted rivers and streams. As the water leaves Lake Erie, it flows into a channel known as the Niagara River.

THE NIAGARA RIVER

Believed to be between 10,000 and 12,000 years old, the Niagara River is short compared to most rivers, covering a distance of only 35 miles (56 km) as it flows from Lake Erie north to Lake Ontario. Yet the river is mighty in terms of volume. The Niagara River carries a mean volume of about 1.5 million gallons (5.6 million L). Along the way, the Niagara River runs rapidly, as the route is steep. From beginning to end, the descent measures 326 feet (99 m). The drop on the upper part of the river, not far from Lake Erie, is only 10 feet (3 m). Just above the falls, the Niagara River gradually drops 50 feet (15 m) before plunging over the falls, which occur about halfway along the river's route.

When the Niagara River exits Lake Erie, it flows in a single channel for about five miles (8 km) before splitting into two channels at Strawberry Island and Grand Island. The eastern channel, which runs along the banks of the United States, continues for about 15 miles (24 km), while the western channel follows the Canadian banks for about 12 miles (19 km). The two channels merge about three miles (5 km) above Niagara Falls at the foot of Grand Island.

Below the falls, the Niagara Gorge extends about seven miles (11 km). The first part of the gorge descends only slightly, about five feet (1.5 m), which makes the area safe for the popular excursion boats that take tourists to the face of Horseshoe Falls. Farther on, the Niagara River drops another 93 feet (28 m) through a narrow area of rapids. Then the river makes a dramatic 90-degree turn through a spectacular whirlpool, shown in the lower color insert on page C-4, where the river turns to the northeast for two miles (3 km) and then north for another 1.5 miles (2.5 km) to Lewiston, New York. The Niagara River then flows north an additional seven miles (11 km), where it drains into Lake Ontario.

Because of the rapids, the river has some secrets. The stretch of Niagara River below the falls has resisted repeated efforts to measure its depth or to map the river bottom. Scientists have attempted to take measurements from on land, in the water, and in the air. They have tried old-fashioned techniques. They have experimented with acoustic measurements. They have attempted to take readings using lasers, but even lasers cannot penetrate to the bottom, partly because the rapids reflect the light and partly because the sediment in the water acts like solid material and blocks the laser. At this point, scientists offer a "best guess" that below the falls, the Niagara River is 49 feet (15 m) deep.

THE WISCONSINAN GLACIAL STAGE

The Wisconsinan glacial stage, when an enormous ice sheet that originated about 75,000 years ago east of Hudson Bay in northern Quebec and Labrador, made three icy sweeps across most of northern North

America. The ice was up to three miles (4.8 km) thick in places, and the immense weight of so much ice left depressions in the earth up to 200 feet (61 m) deep. As the ice melted, the earth rose again, a phenomenon known as *glacial rebound*. Some scientists have shown that the Great Lakes region and the eastern part of the North American continent continues to tilt, rising ever so slightly as part of the glacial rebound.

The first sweep, known as the early Wisconsinan glacial stage, lasted for about 15,000 years before retreating 50,000 years ago. The glaciers of the middle Wisconsinan glacial stage advanced again some 40,000 years ago, keeping much of North America under ice for about 8,000 years. Some 32,000 years ago, the glacier retreated once again.

About 20,000 years ago, the ice sheet of the late Wisconsinan glacial stage advanced, piling ice once again over the entire Niagara Escarpment, a weathered ridge that extends more than 650 miles (1,050 km) from the Door Peninsula in eastern Wisconsin on across Ontario and to Rochester, New York. The escarpment is made up primarily of *dolostone*, a type of limestone originally formed on the bed of an ancient sea that has hardened with the addition of several minerals. The third glacier, like its predecessors, scraped across the surface of the land, pushing boulders and soil in one direction and then pulling them in another. The late Wisconsinan glacial stage sculpted river channels, deepening some to produce lakes. Other riverbeds were dammed with rock and debris, forcing the rivers to find new routes after the glacier receded.

As the ice melted, the water filled four lakes:

- Glacial Lake Algonquin (known today as Lake Superior, Lake Michigan, and Lake Huron)
- Glacial Lake Warren (Lake Erie)
- Glacial Lake Iroquois (Lake Ontario)
- Glacial Lake Tonawanda (in western New York)

Over time, drainage from the upper Great Lakes collected in Lake Erie and spilled into a primary outlet, known today as the Niagara River.

THE ORIGINAL FALLS

Originally, Niagara Falls was located seven miles (11 km) north of its current site. The Niagara River shot over the edge of the Niagara Escarpment and dropped about 35 feet (11 m) into Lake Ontario near the site of present-day Lewiston, New York, and Queenston, Ontario. Geologists estimate that the water flow at the time was about 25 percent of the present flow rate. At the time, Lake Ontario covered the area from Lewiston and Queenston to Niagara-on-the-Lake, a town that sits on the edge of present-day Lake Ontario.

In 1841, a British geologist named Sir Charles Lyell demonstrated that Niagara Falls had formed the Niagara Gorge by eroding upstream from the edge of the escarpment at Queenston and Lewiston to its location at the time of his study. James Hall, an American geologist, concurred, and his independent studies included the first accurate survey of the rim of the early falls. In the early years of the 20th century, a Canadian geologist named J. W. W. "Roy" Spencer discovered the original site of Niagara Falls, which today is known as Roy Terrace at Queenston Heights in Canada.

Like all waterfalls, the original Niagara Falls declined to stay put. Over the last 12,000 years, the falls has receded upstream by wearing away the riverbed, which is made of sedimentary rock and glacial sediment. Underneath a layer of hard *dolostone* are layers of *shale* (a soft, fine-grained sedimentary rock that essentially is consolidated mud and clay), limestone, and sandstone. Over time, the rushing water has broken down the dolostone, sending large chunks of rock to the bottom of the falls. The shale is even easier for the water to destroy, and it crumbles over time as well, undermining and weakening the harder dolostone.

NIAGARA GORGE

In the process of receding, Niagara Falls has sculpted the Niagara Gorge, revealing layers of prehistoric rock formed some 400 million years ago. When the sun hits the layers of rock in the wall of the Niagara Gorge, the layers reflect back shades of beige, rust, lavender, and green, all colors that recount the history of the prehistoric sea that once covered the area. The upper third of the wall is dolostone. Just below the dolostone is shale, which comprises about two-thirds of the gorge wall.

Some of the shale contains thin layers of limestone, sedimentary rock primarily composed of mud, clay, sand, and shells of sea creatures. Some layers of limestone stand alone. Among the 200 fossilized species are worms, clams, snails, species of ancient nautilus and squid, trilobites, crustaceans, corals, sponges, fish, and insects, including centipedes and millipedes. Some of these fossils are shown in the illustration on page 63. Below the fossil-rich shale, additional layers of shale and fine sandstones are found beneath the surface of the river.

A DRAMATIC TURN

In the course of sculpting the Niagara Gorge as Niagara Falls receded upstream, events took a dramatic turn. Some 10,000 to 12,000 years ago, when the last Wisconsinan age glacier was retreating more often than advancing, water from the melting glacier was concentrated in northern Ontario, leaving Lake Erie only half the size it is today and reducing the flow of the Niagara River and the original Niagara Falls. After about 5,000 years, the water once again was routed through southern Ontario, and the river and falls were restored to their former power.

In its continual process of receding upstream, Niagara Falls intersected an old riverbed that the Wisconsinan age glacier had buried and left for dead. Because of the force of the falling water, Niagara Falls easily dropped into this buried gorge, ripped out the boulders and debris and filled the old river bottom with churning rapids.

The result was a 90-degree turn in the path of the river, the current site of a dramatic whirlpool and home of the Whirlpool Rapids. Geologists suggest that the dramatic change in the course of the river took place in just a few days or, at most, a few weeks. The falls then settled in just upriver of the whirlpool and set about the work of receding to the present site.

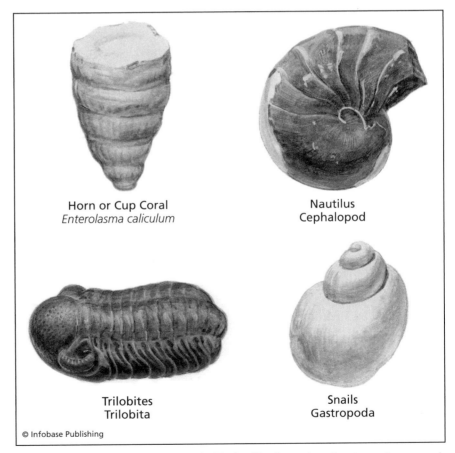

Horn or Cup Coral
Enterolasma caliculum

Nautilus
Cephalopod

Trilobites
Trilobita

Snails
Gastropoda

© Infobase Publishing

The rock in the Niagara River Gorge holds fossilized remains of such species as coral, ancient nautilus, trilobites, and snails.

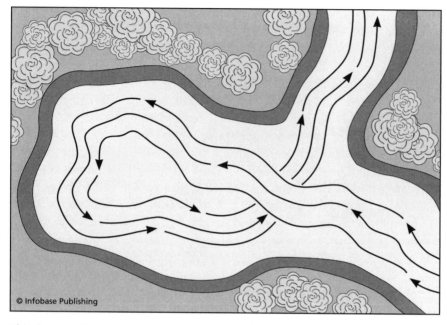

© Infobase Publishing

This drawing illustrates the normal rotation of the dramatic whirlpool in the Niagara River below Niagara Falls.

NIAGARA'S RAPIDS

The Niagara River is home to world-class whitewater rapids said to be the largest series of *standing waves* in North America. A standing wave, also known as a stationary wave, is a wave that remains in a constant position. This results when water is continually moving in the opposite direction of a wave. Standing waves are caused by a great deal of fast-moving water being forced through an area that narrows from a wider place.

Rapids occur at several places along the river. Above the falls, the rapids reach a maximum speed of 25 miles (40 km) per hour. Below the falls, at the Whirlpool Rapids—a place of spectacular natural beauty—the water moves at 30 miles (48 km) per hour. Farther along the river, at the Devil's Hole Rapids, the water has been clocked at 22 miles (36 km) per hour. (All calculations made below the falls took place when the Niagara River was at half flow, its typical volume.) To put these numbers in perspective, consider that rivers most often move at about two to four miles (3 to 6 km) per hour.

Racing whitewater produces *white noise* or *white sound*, a calming, unobtrusive sound at a constant pitch and intensity. Technically, the sound of whitewater rapids is the sound of air, not water. The swiftly moving rapids pull air into the water, which causes bubbles. What people perceive as the roar of the water actually is the sound of air bubbles breaking as they are pushed back out of the water.

Rapids on the rivers in eastern North America are rated on a scale of I to VI. (In western North America, rapids are rated from I to X.) A Class I river has little or no current and small waves. A Class VI river is considered un-navigable. The Whirlpool Rapids, a stretch of the Niagara River some 2.5 miles (4 km) long, is considered a Class VI due to its volume of water, some 757,500 gallons (2,867,137 L) per second. In contrast, the Colorado River—considered a benchmark for whitewater rapids—has a flow of 448,831 gallons (1,699,010 L) per second. Because of the current and the height of the drop, Niagara Falls itself is also considered a Class VI rapid.

THE FUTURE OF NIAGARA FALLS

Geologically speaking, Niagara Falls is racing backward to its source, Lake Erie. Niagara Falls is considered the fastest-moving waterfall on the planet. Between 1842 and 1905, Horseshoe Falls receded upstream at an average rate of about 5.5 feet (1.7 m) per year. Since then humans have interfered with natural erosion. But even with efforts in place to slow the recession of the falls, geologists estimate that Niagara Falls will reach Lake Erie in about 8,000 years. The current rate of erosion at Horseshoe Falls is estimated at one foot (.30 m) per year. Some engineers say the rate possibly could be reduced to one foot (.30 m) every 10 years. The American Falls is eroding about three to four inches (7 to 10 cm) every 10 years.

As the river moves backward, Niagara Falls continues to grow taller. The Cascades Rapids just above the falls stands about 50 feet (15 m) higher than the falls themselves, and once Niagara Falls reaches that ledge, the view will be that much more spectacular. However, some geologists insist that as the falls moves closer to Lake Erie, the water will be reduced to churning rapids, and no longer a true waterfall.

Theories abound regarding the future of the falls. One theory predicts that as Horseshoe Falls continues to head south, in 2,000 years or so it will cut off the river's flow to the American Falls, and Niagara Falls will once again be a single fall. Another theory suggests that because North America's eastern seaboard continues to rise gradually as a result of glacial rebound, eventually water flow to the ocean will slow and reverse. Should that occur, Niagara Falls could cease to exist or would at least be considerably diminished.

SLOWING EROSION

Modern technology, aided by international cooperation, has slowed the rate of erosion at Niagara Falls by diverting water above the falls for use by power plants. The United States and Canada formally agreed in January 1929 to work together to preserve the falls. In 1950, the two countries signed the Niagara River Water Diversion Treaty. The treaty mandates that sufficient amounts of water continue to flow over Niagara Falls "to preserve their scenic value," and the document also addresses the role of water diversion, which provides electrical power and reduces erosion.

The terms of the treaty state that all water in excess of an average of about 972,467 gallons (3,681,188 L) per second be diverted for power generation and that the diverted water be divided equally between the United States and Canada. On the U.S. side, the Robert Moses Niagara Power Plant and the Lewiston Pump Generating Plant house the equipment that converts water to electricity. The plants' counterparts on the Canadian side are the Sir Adam Beck 1 and 2 power plants, also known as power stations. The Robert Moses Niagara Power Plant alone provides 9 to 12 percent of the electricity for the state of New York and processes enough water to provide every U.S. citizen with a glass of water every 12 seconds. All together, the four generating stations can produce about 4.4 GW of power.

The schedule of diversion is as follows: Between April 1 and October 31, 837,818 gallons (3,171,486 L) of water per second are diverted during the day for power. At night less water flows over the falls, as tunnels and canals above the falls capture 1,211,844 gallons (4,587,328 L) of water per second. That same rate of diversion is maintained from November 1 through March 31, sending only about 374,025 gallons (1,415,838 L) of water over the falls. In other words, about 50 percent of the water is diverted during the daylight hours during the spring and summer months, and 75 percent of the water is diverted at night during the summer and all winter long. At peak diversion times, the level of the Niagara River in the gorge drops by about 16 feet (5 m).

The original purpose of diverting water from the falls was to reduce the rate of erosion by sending less water over the falls. The happy result is that the rate of erosion has slowed, and the power generated from the diverted water has benefited citizens on both sides of the Niagara River.

EARLY EFFORTS TO HARNESS THE RIVER

Daniel Joncaire was the first person known to use the energy of Niagara Falls as a source of power. In 1757, Joncaire built a small canal above the falls to power a sawmill. In 1805, Augustus and Peter Porter purchased land around the American Falls from the government of New York. The brothers enlarged the original canal to provide increased power for a *gristmill* (a mill for grinding grain) and tannery. The Niagara Falls Hydraulic Company was chartered in 1853, and the name was later changed to the Niagara Falls Hydraulic Power and Manufacturing Company. Almost 30 years later, under the direction of Jacob Schoellkopf, the company produced sufficient power to send direct current to illuminate Niagara Falls as well as a village nearby named for the falls.

Around this same time, a Serbian-American inventor and researcher named Nikola Tesla discovered the basis of alternating current, which makes the distant transfer of electricity possible. In 1883, the Niagara Falls Power Company (a descendant of Schoellkopf's firm) brought in George Westinghouse to design a system to generate alternating current. At the time, Westinghouse was head of the Westinghouse Electric Company in Pittsburgh. In 1885 Tesla sold Westinghouse the patent rights to his system of alternating-current dynamos, transformers, and motors.

Wealthy businessmen such as J. P. Morgan, John Jacob Astor IV, and the Vanderbilt family all recognized the potential of alternating current and helped to finance Westinghouse's work. By 1896, the Niagara Falls Power Company had constructed giant underground conduits leading to turbines that generated electricity that could be sent all the way to Buffalo, some 20 miles (32 km) from Niagara Falls. Canadian companies also began to harness energy from Niagara Falls. Eventually, the government of Ontario took over all power transmission operations for the province.

ROCKFALLS

Rockfalls represent the biggest threat to the immediate future of both Horseshoe Falls and the American Falls. Rockfalls have particularly plagued the American Falls, which has a great deal of *talus*, or rock debris, at its base. Rockfalls are caused by natural erosion of the dolostone and also by repeated freezing and thawing of water trapped in the rock, which eventually causes it to separate and break. Each time a rockfall occurs, weakened layers of rock beneath are exposed, which makes them more vulnerable to an eventual fall.

The largest single rockfall recorded in the Niagara Gorge occurred at the American Falls on July 28, 1954. A mass of brittle dolostone weighing 185,000 short tons (182,040 metric tons) crashed from Prospect Point and the flank of the falls into the river below. No one was injured. An earlier rockfall at the American Falls, in January of 1931, sent 76,000 short tons (74,784 metric tons) of rock plummeting from the center of the crest. The boulders piled almost halfway up the falls.

Engineers fear that removing the talus might lead to *cavitation*, the phenomenon where small cavities of partial vacuum form in fluid, then rapidly collapse, sending out shock waves and potentially disintegrating nearby rock. The boulders have been left in place at the base of the American Falls as a means of supporting the falls and preventing further erosion of the soft shale layer under the *cap rock*, or top layer, of dolostone.

Concerned about continuous rockfalls—and curious to see what could be done to prevent further incidents—in June 1969 engineers dammed water flowing toward the American Falls, diverting it to the other side of the river and over Horseshoe Falls. In order to help slow erosion and to protect the public at the same time, the engineers bolted faults, shored up part of the bedrock with cement to stabilize the softer rock, and redirected some of the more damaging currents. The engineers installed instruments on Prospect Point, Luna Island, and Terrapin Point to monitor rock movements, and they drilled drainage holes into the limestone to relieve the pressure from the racing water.

The engineers abandoned a plan to remove the talus at the foot of the falls, declaring the effort too expensive and perhaps even foolhardy. In November 1969, the engineers removed the temporary dam and restored the flow of the Niagara River to the American Falls.

Vast amounts of talus lie exposed in this historic photo from June 1969, when engineers dammed water flowing toward the American Falls at Niagara Falls. *(Ron Roels)*

NIKOLA TESLA

Nikola Tesla (1856–1943) was born into a Serbian family on July 9, 1856, in Smiljan, Croatia, the son of an Orthodox priest and a mother said to be highly intelligent though she had little formal schooling. The family considered Tesla something of a dreamer, but he was reared with a penchant for self-discipline and precision. He attended Technical University in Graz, Austria, and the University of Prague, working toward a degree in engineering. His interest in the concept of alternating current developed in Graz, and while in Budapest, Tesla developed plans for an induction motor that eventually would lead to the use of alternating current, or current that can reverse direction. In his free time in 1882, Tesla constructed his first induction motor while working for the Continental Edison Company in Paris.

Nikola Tesla, an eccentric inventor, designed the first hydropower machinery installed at Niagara Falls. *(George Grantham Bain Collection/Library of Congress)*

Two years later, Tesla sailed for America. When he landed in New York, he had a few pennies and some original poems in his pocket, along with calculations for a flying machine. Tesla went to work with Thomas Edison, but the two parted company soon after due to personal and professional clashes. In 1885, Tesla sold the patent rights for his system of alternating-current dynamos, transformers, and motors to George Westinghouse, then head of the Westinghouse Electric Company in Pittsburgh. That transaction brought an end to the ongoing struggle with Edison, who had perfected direct-current systems.

Tesla set up his own laboratory and experimented with the technology that led to the development of X-rays by Wilhelm Röntgen in 1895. He continued with other experiments even as he went to great lengths to allay fears of alternating current. In a public exhibition in his laboratory, Tesla lighted lamps without wires by allowing electricity to flow through his body. He later took his message on the road, speaking to crowds in the United States and elsewhere.

In 1891, Tesla invented the Tesla coil, which is used in radio and television sets and other electronic equipment. That same year, the successful immigrant became a U.S. citizen. Two years later, Westinghouse used Tesla's system of alternating current to light the World's Columbian Exposition in Chicago. That feat won Westinghouse a contract to install the first power machinery at Niagara Falls, machinery that bore Tesla's name and patent numbers.

Throughout the rest of his life, Tesla continued to develop inventions and to make bold predictions for the future. Some people considered him an eccentric—Tesla was terrified of germs and believed he had received extraterrestrial communications—but when he died on January 7, 1943, three Nobel Prize recipients spoke of Tesla at his funeral in New York City as "one of the outstanding intellects of the world who paved the way for many of the technological developments of modern times." Today a memorial statue of Nikola Tesla sits near the Cave of the Winds attraction at Niagara Falls.

ICE JAMS

Efforts to control erosion and harness the power of the river to provide electricity have succeeded, but the Niagara River has presented another challenge: ice jams. One of the most dramatic occurred in 1848, when an ice jam built up in the river between Buffalo and Fort Erie. Acting as a dam, the ice jam held back the flow from Lake Erie for a day, and Niagara Falls dried up completely. Records show that people went for walks in the riverbed and collected timber. Other ice jams of consequence were recorded in 1890, 1899, 1909, 1912, 1938, and 1956.

Ice on the Niagara River originates in Lake Erie, which is large enough to produce up to 10,000 square miles (25,899 km²) of ice. Ice blocks that drop over the falls do not have far to go before the river narrows, and the smaller stream causes the ice to be pushed back upriver. Ice in the river grinds the riverbed, shoves large boulders along, widens the gorge, and otherwise changes the shoreline.

In 1964, the International Joint Commission that governs Niagara Falls approved installation of an ice-control device called an *ice boom*. In place from December to March, the ice boom is a 1.7-mile (2.7-km)-long floating chain of pontoons and steel cable strung across the Niagara River. The ice boom extends from Buffalo, New York, to Fort Erie, Ontario. Though the ice boom keeps ice from clogging the flow of the river, from time to time mounds of ice 50 feet (15 m) high stretch across the river above the water, forming what is known as an *ice bridge*.

On February 24, 1888, a local newspaper reported that 20,000 people were out on an ice bridge, looking at the falls or tobogganing. Entrepreneurs promptly erected shanties on the ice bridge where they sold liquor, photographs, and souvenirs. In February 1912, an ice bridge broke up, causing the deaths of three people. Since then, no one has been allowed on any ice bridge that may form in winter.

IN THE FIELD: TREES ALONG THE NIAGARA RIVER GORGE

The Robert Moses Parkway is a paved road that runs along the crest of the eastern rim of the Niagara Gorge on the U.S. side of the Niagara River. Because the parkway runs parallel to another paved road, government officials are considering removing the public parkway. Government agencies, state park organizations, and a power authority currently own and/or manage the landscape along the gorge, and each of these organizations has expressed a desire to restore the landscape to its natural condition along the gorge and at the river's edge if the parkway is removed.

In 2004, Patricia M. Eckel of the Missouri Botanical Garden investigated the trees along the parkway. Eckel found that the seven-mile (11.3-

km)-long gorge crest (a section between Artpark State Park on the north and Niagara Falls State Park) retains much of the original tree population—a situation that would readily provide a template for environmental restoration if officials decide to remove the Robert Moses Parkway.

Eckel found that red oak, white oak, and pignut hickory trees were dominant in the area. Other common trees included hop-hornbeam, white ash, basswood, sugar maple, black cherry, and tulip. She also found a few examples of black oak and shagbark hickory. Her findings reflect the type of woodland community that seems to occur throughout upstate New York north of the Coastal Lowlands. However, she also found a chestnut oak or two.

In her report, Eckel noted that she saw no coniferous species, though such trees do appear in old photographs of the area. For instance, the white pine appears to be completely absent today, as does the hemlock tree. Both were eliminated from the area during the height of the lumber and leather industries in the early decades of the 20th century. Eckel made her findings available to the agencies and organizations considering removal of the parkway.

PROTECTED LAND

Both the United States and Canada have taken steps to protect Niagara Falls. Prior to 1885, land on both sides of Niagara Falls was privately owned. Developers paid little mind to the natural beauty of the area, and commercial ventures sprang up to take advantage of an increased interest in travel. Legend has it that some entrepreneurs went so far as to charge visitors a fee to peek at Niagara Falls through holes in a fence.

In 1869, famed artist Frederick Church and landscape architect Frederick Law Olmsted discussed with others the need to "free" Niagara. Eventually, a Free Niagara Movement was started, and the state bought land surrounding the falls. On July 15, 1885, the State Reservation at Niagara was dedicated and opened to the public as the first state park in the United States. Three years later, Queen Victoria Niagara Falls Park opened in Ontario on May 14, 1888. Today the Niagara Parks Commission of Canada governs land usage along the course of the Niagara River from Lake Erie to Lake Ontario.

Niagara Falls State Park includes land adjacent to the Niagara River, as well as Goat Island and other, smaller islands by the falls. Both nations restrict development at the falls and along the Niagara River, though both welcome visitors to tourist-friendly attractions on both sides. These efforts ensure that the world-famous Niagara Falls will flow for generations to come.

6

Kahiwa Falls
South Pacific

Twisting and turning in the sun, Kahiwa Falls leaps 2,165 feet (660 m) from a towering sea cliff down the slanted side of a volcanic mountain to the Pacific Ocean on the rugged north shore of Molokai, one of the Hawaiian Islands. The verdant mountains curving along the north shore are the highest sea cliffs in the world, topping out at 3,600 feet (1,100 m). Kahiwa (pronounced *Ka-hee-va*) consists of six drops, with the tallest single drop measuring 600 feet (183 m). The volume of the waterfall has not been calculated, but Kahiwa measures about 25 feet (8 m) wide at peak season, which is in the winter.

Fed by a small stream of the same name, Kahiwa Falls (shown in the upper color insert on page C-5) is the tallest waterfall in Hawaii. In the Hawaiian dictionary, *Kahiwa* translates as "sacred vine," though some say the word also means "the chosen one." Pilipo Solatoiro, a *kupuna*, or elder, on Molokai recalls that Kahiwa is short for *Ka Pali Akahiwa. Ka Pali* translates as "the hill," and *Akahiwa* is the name of a person who lived in the area of the waterfall. Kahiwa Falls drains into Kahiwa Gulch, a deep canyon sculpted over a period of 1 to 2 million years by the earth, the wind, and the rain.

Kahiwa Falls is situated in the wildest and most beautiful part of Molokai, which also happens to be the most remote. The north coast on the eastern side of the island, which stretches 20 miles (32 km) from the Kalaupapa Peninsula to the Halawa Valley, is a pristine range of steep, forested mountains boasting hidden valleys, steep cliffs, and rocky coasts. Geologists suggest that at some point in time much of the northern coast of Molokai collapsed into the ocean, leaving behind the striking cliffs. Huge rocks, some extending for miles, lie at the base of the cliffs under the sea. Kahiwa Falls, which is visible from the sea, is primarily accessible by boat or helicopter, though some experienced hikers have made the 10-mile trek to see it. Residents of Molokai refer

Molokai, home of Kahiwa Falls, has far less commercial development than the other Hawaiian islands. *(Nat Farbman/Time & Life Pictures/Getty Images)*

to the north coast—which is now uninhabited—as the "backside" of the island.

The Hawaiian language has several words for waterfall, including *wailele*, which translates as "leaping water." One of Hawaiian musician and songwriter Dennis Kamakahi's most popular songs commemorates a moment when he glanced up at Kamakou Mountain on Molokai just as the mist was parting, revealing 11 different waterfalls on the mountain. Kamakahi told a friend, "It's like a woman who reveals her beauty to the one she loves. So the mist parts and reveals the beauty of the land." The title of the song, *Wahine 'Ilike*, translates as "Fair-Skinned Woman," and the lyrics speak of "the white mist of Kamakou, revealing the waters of Hina, Goddess of the Moon, who gave birth to Molokai."

Kahiwa is one of hundreds of waterfalls on the north coast of Molokai. Papalaua Falls, some 1,644 feet (501 m) high, flows just east of Kahiwa Falls. The two frequently are misidentified, even on television and in national publications. Molokai is not the only Hawaiian island graced with waterfalls. Among those falls that have names are Kaluahine, Akaka, and Waiilikahi on the island of Hawaii; Honokohau and Waihiumalu on Maui; Kaliuwaa on Oahu; and Waipoo, Awini, Hinalele, and Wailua on Kauai. Many waterfalls in the Hawaiian Islands remain unnamed and unmeasured.

THE HAWAIIAN ISLANDS

Named the 50th state in 1959, Hawaii is unique. The Hawaiian Islands consist of a chain of volcanic mountains that have emerged from the sea, an island paradise built of *extrusive igneous rocks*, or rocks that cooled and solidified at the Earth's surface after bubbling up from far below the Earth's crust. The group of islands, also known as an *archipelago*, stretches across 6,459 square miles (16,728 km²) in the central Pacific Ocean. Author Mark Twain described Hawaii as "the loveliest fleet of islands that lies anchored in any ocean."

Eight major islands and 124 islets, each made up of solidified lava and volcanic debris, form a 1,500-mile (2,414-km) crescent reaching from

Kure Island in the west to the island of Hawaii in the east. The eight major islands are

- Niihau
- Kauai
- Oahu
- Molokai
- Lanai
- Kahoolawe
- Maui
- Hawaii

The islands have a collective population of 1.2 million, which is about the population of Idaho. Honolulu, on the island of Oahu, is the capital city of Hawaii. With a population of 363,000, Honolulu is situated 2,397 miles (3,857 km) from San Francisco to the east and 5,293 miles (8,516 km) from Manila, in the Philippine Islands, to the west.

The name *Hawaii* is said to be a derivation of *Hawaiki*, the former name of one of the Society Islands in the South Pacific, which are part of French Polynesia. The state of Hawaii—often called the Crossroads of the Pacific—is considered economically vigorous, boasting a healthy agriculture and manufacturing base. Hawaii is especially noted for research and development in oceanography, geophysics, astronomy, satellite communications, and biomedicine.

VOLCANIC ORIGINS

Much of the terrain in Hawaii is mountainous. Formed over the past 5 million years by molten rock pouring out from the floor of the Pacific Ocean, the Hawaiian Islands are the tops of volcanic mountains that have risen above sea level. According to Hawaiian folklore, the islands were born when the god Maui stuck his giant fishhook into the ocean and pulled the islands from the seafloor.

Some 80 percent of all volcanic activity takes place below the ocean floor. With each flow of *magma*, or molten rock, from underwater vents deep in the Earth's crust, new land is added. As more magma is added, the land builds up to form new islands. Much more of the magma is added to the seafloor along mid-ocean ridges, which expand the plates, or layers, of the Earth that support the continents. In other areas of the Earth, the plates are recycled as they are shoved deeper and remelt. The landforms are the result of constructive, rather than destructive, eruptions. (Destructive eruptions would blow the mountain apart rather than add acreage.)

Deep below the ocean is the Pacific plate, a layer of the Earth's crust that moves to the northwest about three inches (7.62 cm) each year, carrying the Hawaiian Islands with it. This movement is called *plate tectonics*. In the southeastern part of the Pacific plate is a *hot spot*, an ongoing flow of magma deep in the ocean that pushes up through weak areas in the plate. Hot spots, which cause volcanic eruptions and earthquakes, generally occur near the boundaries, or edges, of plates. This particular hot spot, some 1,988 miles (3,200 km) from the nearest plate boundary, is an exception.

Over 75 million years, nearly 200 islands have been formed as the Pacific plate has moved slowly over the venting hot spot. Many of these volcanic islands are now underwater. The tops of the eight major islands and 124 islets that make up the Hawaiian Islands are above water. Kure, which now sits some 1,500 miles (2,414 km) northwest of its original location, is the oldest of the Hawaiian Islands, formed 30 to 35 million years ago.

The island of Hawaii, also known as the Big Island, is the youngest of all the Hawaiian Islands. Hawaii was formed by five volcanoes known today as

- Kohala
- Mauna Kea
- Hualalai
- Mauna Loa
- Kilauea

Mauna Kea and Mauna Loa are the highest mountains in the state, reaching respective heights of 13,796 feet (4,205 m) and 13,678 feet (4,169 m). In winter, the crests of Mauna Kea and Mauna Loa are frequently covered with snow. Mauna Loa, which translates as "long mountain," is also one of the largest single mountain masses in the world. Measured from the ocean floor, Mauna Loa stands 30,000 feet (9,144 m) tall, and its lava flows occupy more than 2,000 square miles (5,179 km²) of the island.

ACTIVE VOLCANOES

Three of the volcanoes on the island of Hawaii remain active. They are

- Mauna Loa
- Kilauea
- Hualalai

Hualalai has not erupted since 1801, but Mauna Loa and Kilauea are two of the most active volcanoes in the world. Both are located in Volcanoes National Park, which covers nearly 218,000 acres (88,221 ha). Mauna Loa last erupted in 1984. Kilauea, shown in the lower color insert on page C-5, has been erupting continuously since January 1983, allowing scores of tourists to witness molten lava flows, curling steam clouds, and the vast lava fields. This long-term eruption phase has added more than 500 acres of land to the Big Island and, as reported in the

October 2005 issue of *National Geographic*, "oozed enough lava to pave five roads to the moon."

When a volcano erupts, lava (also known as magma or molten rock) ranges from 1,300°F to 2,200°F (700°C to 1,200°C). Lava typically has a flow rate of 100,000 times slower than water. In other words, lava is thick and sluggish, while water runs freely. Dark-colored lava such as basalt, also known as *mafic* lava, forms flows known as *pahoehoe* (pronounced "pah-hoey-hoey") and *aa* (pronounced "ah-ah"). Pahoehoe lava leaves a curving surface in the form of folded fabric or lightly folded rope. In contrast the surface of aa lava is sharp and rough and is characterized by a layer of loose, irregular fragments known as clinker. Some lava flows from the vent originally as pahoehoe, changing to aa on the route down the side of the volcano. Lava that leaves the vent as aa does not change.

One active volcano, currently under the sea about 20 miles (32 km) off the southeast coast of the island of Hawaii, may someday be another link in the chain of Hawaiian Islands. Loihi Seamount (a *seamount* is an active underwater volcano) rises 17,000 feet (5,182 m) above the ocean floor and is about 3,000 feet (914 m) below sea level. Geologists speculate that Loihi could emerge from beneath the waves in about 60,000 years.

CLIMATE OF HAWAII

Rainfall on the islands varies dramatically, depending on the region. On Molokai summer runs from May through October, and winter prevails the other six months of the year. The average temperature on Molokai ranges from 75°F to 85°F (23.8°C to 29.4°C), and the average annual rainfall is 30 inches (76 cm). All the Hawaiian Islands have a dry side to the west and a wet side to the east. Rain is most plentiful in the mountains.

On the island of Kauai, Mount Waialeale—often called the wettest spot on Earth—has recorded an annual average rainfall of 444 inches (1,128 cm) over a 60-year period, the highest long-term median on record. In contrast, on the island of Hawaii, the average annual rainfall at Kawaihae is only 8.7 inches (22 cm). In recent years, both Maui and the island of Hawaii have experienced mild droughts.

Throughout the islands, rainfall is heaviest in mountainous areas, where the frequent showers swell small streams that carve out grooves, ridges, and many V-shaped valleys. When the volcanic islands were young, few streams coursed down the mountains, as rain easily penetrated the porous volcanic rock. The water collected in subterranean chambers under the surface of the mountain. Over time thick soil—made up of volcanic ash, gravel, rotted vegetation, crumbling lava, and sand and dust carried by the wind—formed. With soil to carry them, streams took hold aboveground, and waterfalls developed wherever those streams were interrupted as they coursed down the sides of mountains.

J. TUZO WILSON

In 1963, J. Tuzo Wilson (1908–93), a Canadian geophysicist, devised the theory of hot spots, the continuous magma flows deep in the ocean that push up through weak areas in the Earth's plates. Wilson's theory suggested that the Hawaiian Islands and other volcanic island chains such as the Galápagos Islands may have formed due to the movement of a plate over a stationary hot spot. His hypothesis explained how active volcanoes could occur far from the nearest plate boundary.

Wilson hypothesized that "the distinctive linear shape" of the Hawaiian Island–Emperor Seamounts chain is a result of the Pacific Plate moving over a stationary hotspot located beneath the present-day position of the island of Hawaii. Heat from this hotspot, Wilson suspected, produced a persistent source of magma that rises and then erupts to form an active seamount. Repeated eruptions over time cause the seamount to grow and eventually emerge above sea level as an island volcano.

The continuous movement of the plate eventually carries the island volcano away from the hotspot. When the source of magma is thus removed, further formation of the island volcano desists. As evidence, Wilson pointed out that the oldest volcanic rocks on Kauai (the northwestern most inhabited Hawaiian island) are about 5.5 million years old and are deeply eroded. By comparison the oldest-exposed rocks on Hawaii—the island still positioned over the hotspot—are less than 0.7 million years old, and new volcanic rock is continually being formed.

Long before Wilson spoke up, before any scientific studies were done, the ancient Hawaiians had noticed the differences in erosion, soil formation, and vegetation among the islands. They believed that Niihau and Kauai, the northwestern islands, were older than Maui and Hawaii in the southeast. As part of Hawaii's oral tradition, this theory was handed down from generation to generation as one of the legends of Pele, the fiery goddess of volcanoes.

The legend is that Pele originally lived on Kauai. When her older sister Namakaokahai, the goddess of the sea, attacked her, Pele fled to Oahu. Next Pele moved to Maui and, finally, to Hawaii, where she now lives in the Halemaumau Crater at the summit of Kilauea. Pele's flight from Kauai to Hawaii is an allegory for the eternal struggle between the growth of volcanic islands from eruptions and their later erosion by ocean waves, and that allegory is consistent with geologic evidence obtained centuries later.

In the early 1960s, Wilson's theory of hot spots was so controversial that none of the major international scientific journals would publish his hypothesis. The *Canadian Journal of Physics* finally published the manuscript in 1963. Subsequently, hundreds of studies proved Wilson's theory to be correct, and his work represented a landmark in the study of plate tectonics. In 1965, Wilson published a new theory, proposing that a third type of plate boundary must connect the oceanic ridges and trenches, because some boundaries end abruptly and transform into major faults that slip horizontally. (An example of such a transform-fault boundary is the San Andreas Fault Zone.)

Born on October 24, 1908, Wilson served as a professor of geophysics at the University of Toronto from 1946 until 1974. He made his valuable contributions to the plate tectonics theory when he was in his mid-50s. After he retired, Wilson became the director of the Ontario Science Centre. He traveled and lectured until his death on April 15, 1993. Today the U.S. Geological Survey reports that scientists once again are debating the character of hot spots.

Rain, sea, and wind have all sculpted the Hawaiian Islands, shaping the mountains into craggy silhouettes made of steep cliffs, collapsed craters (also known as *calderas*), deep valleys, and rolling coastal plains. The shoreline is made up of volcanic lava edged with coral reefs, and the many sandy beaches of Hawaii are a result of coral and shells crushed by pounding waves.

FLORA AND FAUNA

Many plants and animals have evolved into separate species as a result of the isolation of the Hawaiian Islands, but many native species have been pushed out by introduced species. Today government officials and ecologists are working to save many of the 284 endangered plant species and the nene goose, the state bird of Hawaii.

Maui is home to the endangered nene goose and the rare silversword plant. Kauai has the largest number of native bird species in Hawaii, primarily because it is the only major island that lacks the mongoose, a carnivorous mammal that eats the eggs of ground-nesting birds. The most common trees in Kauai are the ohia lehua, koa, guava, kiawe, and kukui. Ohia lehua, the predominant tree in the rain forests on the islands, is endemic, or native, to Hawaii. A particularly hard wood, ohia lehua was used for some of the ties that connected the first railroad across the United States. Due to overgrazing, the island of Lanai has recorded the greatest loss of native forests, plants, and birds.

Molokai boasts two dominant species of trees, including ohia lehua in the rain forests and kiawe in the dryer areas. Pandanus trees also grow on the island. Kukui forests and the fast-growing guava, which is considered a pest plant, grow along the banks of streams.

More than 250 species of Hawaiian plants—most of them found only in the islands—grow in the rain forest of Kamakou Preserve, which is located near Kamakou Mountain, the highest mountain on Molokai. Managed by the Nature Conservancy and the State Department of Land and Natural Resources, the 2,774-acre (1,122-ha) preserve is open to visitors only once a month.

Among the plants in the preserve are alani, which is in the same family as common citrus fruits; hapu'u, or Hawaiian tree fern; and the ohia lehua, which boasts brilliant red, yellow, or orange blossoms and is the signature tree of Hawaii's rain forests. This particular rain forest is very important to the island, as it provides more than 60 percent of the water used on Molokai. Just outside the forest on the preserve is an ancient bog that has a garden of bonsai plants with bright red lehua blossoms. Many rare plant species, some extinct in the wild, are on display in the Foster Garden and the Lyon Arboretum, both on Oahu.

Two native mammals live on the island of Hawaii. The hoary bat is found in Kokee State Park, and the Hawaiian monk seal can sometimes be seen on isolated beaches. Wild horses roam in Waipio Valley, and feral cattle graze on the slopes of Mauna Kea. A population of brush-tailed rock wallabies brought in and accidentally released in 1916, lives on the Big Island. Zoologists are especially interested in the wallabies because they are thought to be extinct in their native Australia. Wild pigs, goats, sheep, and black-tailed deer—all introduced species—are found on all the islands. Birds in the Hawaiian Islands include the red-tailed tropic bird, the Hawaiian hawk, the Maui parrotbill, the pueo (a relative of the North American short-eared owl), and the o'u, which is highly endangered.

EARLY HISTORY OF HAWAII

Captain James Cook, an English explorer and navigator, landed on Kauai in January 1778, some 1,128 years after settlers first arrived on Molokai. Cook was the first European to "discover" Hawaii, which he named the Sandwich Islands. Europeans who ventured to the islands after Cook's visit reported that King Kamehameha I used European military technology and weapons in his struggle to seize control of the islands. Born between 1748 and 1761 in North Kohala on the island of Hawaii, Kamehameha is still revered as Hawaii's greatest statesman, warrior, and king, though a long line of monarchs followed him.

Early in the 19th century, the U.S. whaling fleet out of Nantucket, Massachusetts, moved its winter operations to Lahaina, Maui, in what was known as the kingdom of Hawaii. Explorers, traders, and adventurers followed the whalers, and missionaries arrived on Maui soon afterward. By 1820, the first of 15 groups of missionaries had arrived from New England. By 1850, Maui looked much like a town in Massachusetts, dotted with frame houses, horse-drawn vehicles, schools, churches, taverns, and shops. The Americans introduced the Polynesians to a written language, working skills, and Protestant and Roman Catholic religious beliefs—changing Hawaiian culture forever.

In 1893, American businessmen struck a particularly devastating blow to the kingdom of Hawaii. In an effort to protect industrial profits in the exportation of goods (such as sugar) to the United States, prominent businessmen organized the Committee of Safety, a 13-member council eager to depose Queen Liliuokalani. Politically savvy, these men arranged for assistance from American troops. The USS *Boston* landed in Honolulu and removed the queen from her palace at gunpoint. She was arrested, tried by the American Judge Advocate General's Corps, and imprisoned in her home. On November 23, 1993, President Bill Clinton signed into law a formal apology for the illegal action.

THE ISLAND OF MOLOKAI

Molokai, the third oldest of the Hawaiian Islands, is the home of Kahiwa Falls. Formed by three different volcanic mountains that rose from the sea, Molokai is said to be 2 million years old. The fifth largest of the Hawaiian Islands, Molokai lies east of Oahu across the Kaiwi Channel and northwest of Maui across the Pailolo Channel. The island is 40 miles (65 km) long and about seven miles (11 km) wide, covering about 261 square miles (675 km²), with 88 miles (141 km) of unspoiled coastline.

Molokai is shaped like a shark, with the small Kalaupapa Peninsula on the north shore serving as the dorsal fin. The island formed in stages, as shown in the illustration on page 81. In the Tertiary Period between 65 million and 2 million years ago, two separate volcanoes—the West Molokai Volcano and the East Molokai Volcano—rose above sea level. The volcanic mountains continued to grow, and a crater formed on East Molokai Volcano. Over time the two islands merged and the West Molokai Volcano became extinct. Part of the single island was submerged in the late Pliocene or early Pleistocene Epoch (some 2 million years ago), separating the two sides of the island. By the late Pleistocene, some 10,000 years ago, the two islands had merged once again and a minor volcano had arisen on the north shore, forming what later would be called Kalaupapa Peninsula. All volcanic activity ceased over time.

The arid western portion of Molokai is called Mauna Loa, where the highest peak is Puu Nana, which stands 1,381 feet (421 m) high. The forested eastern portion of Molokai is home to Kamakou Mountain, which is 4,970 feet (1,515 m) high. Kahiwa Falls is on the northern edge of the eastern side of the island, near Halawa, a deep agricultural gorge some four miles (6.4 km) long and half a mile (0.8 km) wide. A connecting ridge, also known as a saddle, rises 400 feet (120 m) high to link the two portions of the island. The ancient name of the island is Molokai Pule O'o, which translates as "Molokai of the Powerful Prayer."

HISTORY OF MOLOKAI

The first settlers on Molokai arrived about 650 C.E. The earliest settlers came from the Marquesas Islands, some 2,000 miles (3,218 km) away. Some 500 years later, others migrated to Molokai from Tahiti and elsewhere in the South Pacific, arriving in double-hulled canoes. The oldest-known settlement on Molokai was in what is now known as Halawa Valley, at the eastern end of the island. Settlers lived well, with freshwater from the mountains, fertile land for farming, and the riches of the ocean. The early people of Molokai did not have a written language, but they did have chants that relayed epic tales of events, battles, and family histories and that were passed from generation to generation.

In the early days, Molokai was renowned for its religious leaders. Lanikaula, a famous prophet on Molokai, received pilgrims from all the islands during the 1500s. Other religious leaders on Molokai were no-

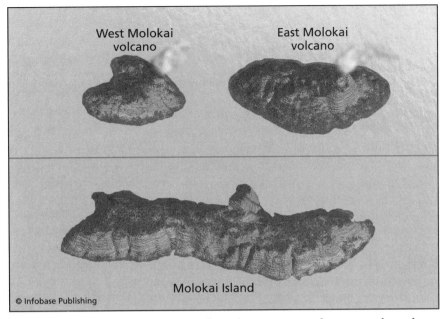

The island of Molokai formed in stages from three separate volcanoes, as shown here.

torious for sorcery. Laka, goddess of the hula, introduced the dance on Molokai, an occasion still celebrated on the island each May. The graceful dance is said to combine the fluidity of water with the spark of fire.

In 1786, Captain George Dixon dropped anchor off Molokai's coast. Dixon and his crew were the first Europeans to visit the island. The Reverend Harvey Hitchcock established a Protestant mission on the eastern side of Molokai in 1832. Today a white marble headstone marks Hitchcock's grave on a hill east of the remains of the church.

The population of Molokai has fluctuated significantly in the past 200 years. In ancient times, the island was an affluent community, with a prosperous stone quarry. Even the north shore had settlements, primarily of fishermen and taro farmers and their families. In 1900, some 70 people still lived in Pelekunu Valley, but within 20 years, they had all left the area. By the early 1900s, poor soil and shortage of freshwater caused many people to leave Molokai for the other islands, which were more developed and offered better opportunities to make a living.

The Hawaiian Homes Act, passed in 1921, brought new residents to Molokai. Congress developed the act, a homesteading program to place native Hawaiians (defined as those with 50 percent or more Hawaiian heritage) on lands in Hawaii designated for that purpose. Some 200,000 acres (80,937 ha) were deemed "available lands" under the act. At first a lack of water accounted for slow development, but with the growth of the pineapple industry, several villages sprang up after 1923. In the 1970s and 1980s, pineapple growers faced stiff competition from abroad, and many growers shut down their businesses.

Today Molokai has a population of just over 7,000. More than 2,500 of the island's inhabitants are more than 50 percent Hawaiian, and the islanders pride themselves on maintaining a slower pace of life than that of the other islands. Kaunakakai, a three-block-long village on the south coast, is the largest town. Coffee and sweet potatoes are among the significant exports, and about one-third of the western half of the island is a cattle ranch. In recent years, visitors numbered about 80,000 annually. Many visitors, favoring the upscale hotels available on the other islands, come to Molokai just for the day—some of them hoping for a look at Kahiwa Falls.

EXILE ON KALAUPAPA PENINSULA

At one time, the Kalaupapa Peninsula on the north shore of Molokai was home for individuals diagnosed with Hansen's disease, also known as *leprosy*, a chronic, infectious disease that affects the nerves, skin, and eyes. The first documented case in Hawaii occurred in 1848. The disease is believed to have spread to Hawaii from China. Because leprosy spread easily and there was no cure for it, officials wanted an isolated area to house those with the contagious, disfiguring disease.

The first infected individuals were shipped to the Kalaupapa Peninsula early in 1866. In addition to grappling with the disease, the people had to live in rock enclosures, caves, and shacks built of sticks and dried leaves. No freshwater was available. Records show that ships delivering ill individuals did not want to land, so sometimes those with leprosy were told to jump overboard and swim to shore through the waves. Crew members then would toss supplies into the water and count on the currents to carry them ashore.

In 1873, a Catholic missionary priest from Belgium, Father Damien deVeuster, arrived at the settlement at the age of 33. He built homes and churches, secured medical services and funding for supplies from the government in Honolulu, and served as a surrogate parent to his patients. Father Damien died in 1889 of leprosy.

Some 8,000 people were torn from their families and essentially exiled to the Kalaupapa Peninsula, never to see their loved ones again. In the 1940s, drugs were developed that put individuals with the disease in remission, and leprosy was removed from the list of contagious diseases. Fewer than 100 patients remain today on the peninsula, which also houses an administration building, post office, bookstore, fire station, and hospital. The peninsula is a National Historic Site, and access is strictly regulated in this historic part of Molokai.

The existence of Whiskeytown Falls, a 400-foot (121-m)-tall waterfall in the Whiskeytown National Recreation Area near Redding, California, was first reported in 2005. *(National Park Service)*

Angel Falls, which crashes down from a rocky mesa in southeast Venezuela, is the tallest waterfall in the world. *(Mark Cosslet/National Geographic/Getty Images)*

On sunny days, rainbows lend a bit of magic to the dramatic Victoria Falls, located on the border between Zambia and Zimbabwe. *(Karlien du Plessis/www. shutterstock.com)*

Ponderosa pine and incense cedars frame the path to Yosemite Falls in Yosemite National Park in California. *(Patricia Corrigan)*

Yosemite Valley boasts a seven-mile (11-km)-long stretch of majestic granite cliffs carved by glaciers. *(Patricia Corrigan)*

Gavarnie Falls occurs in the Cirque de Gavarnie, a semicircle of mountainous cliffs at the upper end of a valley in the Pyrenees Mountains in France. *(Lee Brown)*

Niagara Falls consists of the American Falls (foreground) in the United States and the mist-clouded Horseshoe Falls (center), which is in Ontario, Canada. *(Patricia Corrigan)*

The Whirlpool Rapids, below Niagara Falls on the Niagara River, cause roiling water where the river makes a 90-degree turn. *(Patricia Corrigan)*

Flowing down the highest sea cliffs in the world, Kahiwa Falls is one of many waterfalls on the north coast of the Hawaiian island of Molokai. *(Paul Chesley/Getty Images)*

The Kilauea volcano, on the island of Hawaii, has been spewing molten lava and curling steam clouds continuously since January 1983. *(Michael Schofield/www.shutterstock.com)*

Some 275 different waterfalls make up Iguaçu Falls, an imposing natural wonder that occurs on the border between Argentina and Brazil. *(Dario Diament/www.shutterstock.com)*

A pedestrian bridge spans Multnomah Falls at the base of the first tier of the waterfall, located in the Columbia River Gorge in Oregon. *(Harry H. Marsh/www.shutterstock.com)*

Extending 80 miles (128 km) between Oregon and Washington, the Columbia River Gorge is the only sea-level passage through the Cascade Mountains. *(Shawna Caldwell/www.shutterstock.com)*

Located in southwestern India, Jog Falls consists of four distinct cascades of water that stretch across 1,550 feet (472 m) of rock wall. *(K. L. Kamat/Kamat's Potpourri)*

Cumberland Falls, also known as "The Niagara of the South," occurs on the Cumberland River in the southeastern part of Kentucky. *(Courtesy www. kentuckytourism.com)*

Eagle Falls developed along the Cumberland River as Cumberland Falls retreated up the valley. *(Kentucky Geological Survey)*

IN THE FIELD: NATIONAL PARK SERVICE STUDY

The National Park Service is studying an area on the north shore of Molokai to determine the feasibility of adding more land to Kalaupapa National Historical Park, founded in 1980. Much of the land in the 10,700-acre (4,330-ha) park is managed, though not owned, by the National Park Service. The Department of Hawaiian Home Lands and the state's departments of Health, Transportation, and Land & Natural Resources own the land.

The land under consideration for annexation—some 24,000 acres (9,712 ha)—includes the north shore cliffs from Kalaupapa to the Halawa Valley, an area that includes the Pelekunu and Wailau Valleys and their watersheds and the upper watershed of the Halawa Stream. All of the land is within the boundary of the North Shore Cliffs National Natural Landmark, and the reason for annexation is to place the area within the national park system.

A HIDDEN TREASURE

Isolated as it is on the harsh north coast of Molokai, Kahiwa Falls is perhaps the least-visited waterfall of those in this book. The sea is calmest off the north shore of the island in summer, but Kahiwa Falls runs at its fullest in winter, when the ocean is far more volatile. Waves routinely slam 50 feet (15 m) high or higher up the side of the cliffs, and the windy seas are treacherous, so boats are unable to bring tourists to the north shore. Even commercial fishermen are reluctant to pause near the steep rocky cliffs on the north coast in winter, when the slightest change in the weather could keep them from reaching a safe harbor.

Some people may say, then, that the natural charms and the spectacular setting of Kahiwa Falls are wasted. Others may take comfort in the existence of inaccessible beauty.

7

Iguaçu Falls
South America

Iguaçu Falls, perhaps the most dramatic of all waterfalls, surpasses the competition in sheer numbers of cascades. True to its name, which translates as "great water," Iguaçu Falls consists of 275 separate streams all rushing over a horseshoe-shaped cliff that stretches 1.7 miles (2.7 km) along the border between Brazil and Argentina in South America. To put that in perspective, this veritable festival of waterfalls is nearly three times wider than Niagara Falls and is 3,476 feet (1,059 m) wider than Victoria Falls in Africa.

Most of Iguaçu Falls is in Argentina, but the Brazilian side is said to offer a panoramic view of all 275 waterfalls plunging over the cliff. Locals joke that "Argentina puts on the show and Brazil charges for the view." Individual waterfalls at Iguaçu Falls range from 200 to 269 feet (60 to 82 m) high. In the course of the drop, many of the falls veer around protruding rocky ledges, and on sunny days, numerous rainbows are present as a result of the deflection of the water at each change in direction.

The mean annual rate of flow of Iguaçu Falls is about 463,792 gallons (1,755,643 L) per second. The highest volume recorded occurred after heavy rains in 1992, when the rate of flow rose to 7,660,987 gallons (28,999,990 L) per second. From November to March—the rainy season—the flow of Iguaçu Falls has been measured as high as 3,366,233 gallons (12,742,578 L) per second. From August to October, which is the dry season, the flow is considerably less. On rare occasions—for a week or more every several decades—drought can cause Iguaçu Falls to dry up completely.

Iguaçu Falls, sometimes spelled "Iguazu" or "Iguassu," occurs on the Iguaçu River 14 miles (23 km) above its confluence with the Alto Paraná River. Some 2.4 miles (4 km) wide just above the falls, the Iguaçu River divides into many different streams because of the presence of numerous wooded, rocky islands where the river nears the edge of the Paraná Plateau, a thick layer of hard rock. In the rainy season, some of the smaller islands become submerged, which leads to fewer individual cascades. Much of the year, 14 broad streams merge and send about half the river's flow into a narrow, semicircular chasm known as *Garganta do Diabo*, Portuguese for "Devil's Throat." A deafening roar emerges from this particular throat, a roar often described as "an ocean plunging into an abyss." A curtain of mist 500 feet (150 m) high rises from the bottom of Devil's Throat.

Rocky ledges abound at Iguaçu Falls, where 275 waterfalls are gradually eroding the basalt. *(Dario Diament/www.shutterstock.com)*

In addition to Devil's Throat, 18 of the individual waterfalls—many of them visible in the upper color insert on page C-6—are considered major drops, and some of them also have names. Among them are Dos Hermanas, Bozzetti, San Martín, Escondido, Rivadavia, Benjamin Constant, Deodoro, and Floriano. The Guarani named the collective falls "Iguaçu." In the 16th century, a Spanish explorer renamed the spectacle Santa Maria Falls, but the name never took hold.

FORMATION OF THE FALLS

Plate tectonic forces, or movement below the Earth's crust, separated South America from Africa some 200 million years ago. One hundred million years ago, eruptions caused basaltic lava to push up through weakened chasms, creating deep channels, or *spillways*. Three of these channels, covered by water, contributed to the formation of Iguaçu Falls. The larger channel stands between 462 and 590 feet (141 and 180 m) high. A smaller channel measures between 380 and 462 feet (116 and 141 m) high, and the third is smaller still. Water tumbles down three steps in these channels, forming two areas of higher falls and one of smaller cascades.

Movement of the continental plates has created *faults*, or vertical cracks, at Iguaçu Falls, which flows over *basalt*. The most common form of lava, basalt is *extrusive igneous rock*, or rock that has crystallized from liquid magmas that reached the surface and then were vented as volcanic lavas. Basalt is dark, fine-grained, and heavy. Petrobrás, the Brazilian petroleum company, reports finding layers of basalt more than 5,000 feet (1,524 m) deep in the Paraná Basin, which is one of the largest flood-basalt provinces in the world. At Iguaçu Falls, the land consists of eight to 10 layers of basalt that collectively measure 3,250 feet (991m) deep.

The basalt in the Paraná Basin contains some of the world's largest-known *vesicles*, or preserved gas bubbles. Bubbles of gas occur when magma rises and expands, just as bubbles of gas spill into a glass when a carbonated drink is opened and poured. The bubbles of gas in magma form hollow tubes as the magma cools. The tubes create an environment that allows crystals of amethyst (crystalline quartz) to form. Amethyst also is known as purple quartz because of its color. The color comes from trace amounts of ferric iron in the water that passes through the vesicles.

Most vesicles range in diameter from fractions of an inch (2.5 cm) to a few inches (6 cm), but the vesicles in the Paraná Basin range up to .6 mile (.97 km) in length. Amethyst is resistant to weathering and has remained in place even where weathering has broken down the basalt into weak, clay-rich soil. Gem collectors around the world value the vesicles, which occur as *geodes* or hollow, spherical rocks with crystals lining the interior wall. Miners in Brazil quarry the geodes from the rock in the Paraná Basin.

© Infobase Publishing

Geodes are hollow, spherical rocks with crystals lining the interior wall.

Myths and legends also exist regarding the formation of Iguaçu Falls. The Caingangue, a native tribe that once lived on the borders of the Iguaçu River, believed that the falls were created from the tears shed as a result of a tragic love story that involved the daughter of a tribal chief. Another legend tells of an angry local river god who created the Iguaçu gorge as his grave. The god was said to be angry when a local tribesman carried off a virgin who was to have been sacrificed.

THE GUARANI

The Guarani, the first people to settle in eastern Paraguay and nearby areas in Brazil and Argentina, were also the first to know of Iguaçu Falls. The Guarani lived like other native residents of the tropical forests. The women of the tribe maintained fields of corn, sweet potatoes, and cassava, a plant grown for its starchy roots. (Cassava is also known as yucca or manioc.) The men hunted and fished. The tribe, made up of 60 or more individuals, would move to a different part of the forest to begin again every five or six years after the resources in one area were depleted. Guarani warriors were vicious and allegedly captured and ate their enemies. By the late 20th century, the Apapocuva were believed to be the last of the scattered Guarani communities in northeastern Paraguay.

Spanish explorers searching for gold and silver in Paraguay who settled on small ranches were said to keep harems of Guarani women. Over time their descendants formed the basis of the rural population of modern Paraguay. Most of the 1 million peasants who live along the Paraguay River around Asunción today speak a language called Guarani, and the country prides itself on upholding the continuity of Guarani customs and language. Because of the early Spanish colonization, few true aboriginal customs have survived, and the language is considerably altered.

IGUAÇU NATIONAL PARK

In 1897, a Brazilian army officer named Edmundo de Barros first promoted the establishment of a national park at Iguaçu Falls. As a result, two parks were founded, Iguazu National Park in Argentina in 1934 and Iguaçu National Park in Brazil in 1939. Together with the Uruguai Provincial Park in Argentina, the three parks form one of the most extensive remaining tracts of inland Atlantic rain forest and represent the only remnant of a forest that once covered the western part of the Brazilian states of Paraná, São Paulo, Santa Catarina, and Rio Grande do Sul.

Officials at both national parks pledged to preserve the vegetation, wildlife, and scenic beauty of the area. In 1984, the park in Argentina was designated a World Heritage site by the United Nations Educational, Scientific and Cultural Organization. Two years later, the park in Brazil was granted World Heritage status.

Iguaçu Falls is in the middle of the park in Brazil, which covers 420,291 acres (170,086 ha). The 275 waterfalls that make up Iguaçu Falls are surrounded by a rain forest. Summers are hot and humid, and winters are dry and cool. The annual average temperature is 74.8°F (23.8°C), but the temperature can be as high as 109°F (43°C) in the summer and as low as 23°F (−5°C) in the winter. The rain forest, as well as the fauna and flora in it, benefit greatly from the humidity provided by the falls.

The vegetation in the park is rich and varied. A family of water plants that favors rushing water is found on the ledges of the falls. Orchids, mosses, ferns, bamboos, and palms can all be seen from the walkways at the falls, all thriving in the moist air.

Various bird species—many of them endangered—inhabit the rain forest and fly among the waterfalls. Birds commonly seen at the site include parrots, toucans, gray-bellied spine tails, hawk eagles, ground doves, dark-billed cuckoos, screech owls, cardinals, finches, and swallows. At least 500 species of butterflies live in the area, including the electric blue morpho and the poisonous red and black heliconius. Some days hundreds of butterflies can be seen hovering in the air.

Red brocket deer, white-eared opossums, tapirs, and monkeys are commonly seen in Iguaçu National Park, as are coati, four-legged mam-

THE ROAD TO TROUBLE

In May 1997, some 800 people entered Iguaçu National Park in Brazil and began reopening Colono Road, an old colonial passage that had connected two local towns before the road was closed in 1986. Built in 1954 by the Paraná government, the road extended some 11 miles (18 km) through the park, connecting Capanema and Madianeira counties outside the park's boundaries.

The citizens, equipped with the large machinery needed to do the job, claimed that closing the road had caused economic problems. They wanted the road opened to make the parklands more accessible for hunting, fishing, and felling trees. They succeeded in their mission because political pressures forced conservation authorities to look the other way. For a time, the citizens imposed a tax on anyone who wished to use the road, and they also prohibited park employees from working to maintain the area.

In response, ICOMOS/Brasil, an international nongovernmental organization of professionals dedicated to the conservation of the world's historic monuments and sites, called on government authorities and international organizations to protest the situation. Pressure from agencies such as the World Heritage Committee—an official United Nations Educational, Scientific and Cultural Organization (UNESCO)—eventually forced Brazilian governmental authorities to close the road in June 2001, citing the threat the road represented to the biological integrity of the park. Authorities established a police station at the entrance to the road, tore up the rebuilt road, and planted 25,000 seedlings to replace the cleared vegetation.

In October 2003, some 300 citizens again invaded the park with bulldozers. They broke down restraining fences, destroyed the local office of the Brazilian Environmental Agency, and set about reopening the road. The World Wildlife Fund (WWF), an international conservation agency, immediately registered its disapproval. "This misguided action threatens the park, its ecological health and millions of people who benefit from the services it provides," Guillermo Castilleja said in a statement. Castilleja is the WWF vice president for Latin America and the Caribbean, areas where the WWF has been actively involved since 1971.

Castilleja's statement noted that reopening the road would divide the park in two and interrupt "a tri-national forest corridor" that connects with a large block of Atlantic Forest, one of the most biologically important and threatened ecosystems in the world. Nearly 28 million people in the region benefit from the forest's ecological services, including watershed protection and hydroelectric power, and the regional economy owes much to the scenic beauty of Iguaçu Park.

The area in question encompasses two natural World Heritage Sites, two UNESCO Biosphere Reserves, two national parks, and several provincial parks and private reserves. Castilleja called for protection of the park, of the biodiversity and ecological health of the area, and emphasized that the road must not be allowed "to sever the lifeline to the region's health and prosperity."

In 2004, the road was closed once again when newly elected governors of Iguaçu National Park took office. In a private communication written late in 2005, Monica Echeverría, communications coordinator with the WWF's Latin America and Caribbean program, noted that the situation seemed to be under control. She credited the Iguaçu National Park management, which was working closely with the communities of the surrounding areas on environmental and education ecotourism.

mals that look like raccoons but have longer tails and pointy noses. Iguanas are ubiquitous, as is the tegu lizard, which is an endangered species. The white-lipped peccary (a wild pig), southern river otter, jaguar, ocelot, and puma are harder to find. The cats are nocturnal, and the wild animals are easily camouflaged in the dense forest.

IGUAÇU RIVER

Iguaçu Falls is the most spectacular of all the waterfalls along the Iguaçu River basin, which extends a total of about 38,525 square miles (99,779 km²). The river's source is located in the Serra do Mar near Curitiba, a large city at an altitude of about 3,937 feet (1,200 m) on the eastern edge of the Brazilian Highlands, which descend to the Atlantic coast. *Serra do Mar* is Portuguese for "mountain range of the sea." Ranges in the Highlands average between 2,600 and 3,000 feet (800 and 900 m). Locals know the Iguaçu River as the Rio Grande de Curitiba. The river flows west for some 807 miles (1,300 km) across the Paraná Plateau, which is made up of a thick layer of hard basalt.

Along the route, the river receives water from about 30 other rivers and streams, widening significantly with each addition. The route is not flat. The Iguaçu River features some 70 waterfalls (none as spectacular as Iguaçu Falls) and descends about 2,650 feet (807 m) in its travels. Rapids begin about two miles (3.5 km) above Iguaçu Falls.

Below the falls, the Iguaçu River continues through a narrow gorge. Formed by the river, the gorge is 164 feet (50 m) wide, with the walls measuring from 65 to 328 feet (20 to 100 m) high. The gorge carries the river to its confluence with the Alto Paraná River, where the borders of Brazil, Paraguay, and Argentina converge.

The Alto Paraná River begins in the mountains outside Rio de Janeiro, Brazil, and travels some 680 miles (1,094 km). The many waterfalls along the way make the river as un-navigable as the Iguaçu River. After the Alto Paraná flows down a southern slope of the Brazilian Highlands, it cuts through a mountain pass, once the site of the Guaira Falls, which once boasted eight times the water volume of Niagara Falls. Just beyond the falls, the river expanded into a lake 2.5 miles (4 km) wide and 4.5 miles (7.2 km) long. The waterfall and the lake were both submerged with the construction of the Itaipu Dam in 1982.

After the Iguaçu River joins the Alto Paraná, it proceeds southwest, twisting in its rocky bed along the border between Paraguay and Argentina. At Posadas, Argentina, the river turns to the west, weaving its way among islands and basalt outcroppings and moved along by frequent areas of rapids. The Alto Paraná River eventually joins the Rio de la Plata, which spills into the Atlantic Ocean on the east coast of South America between Uruguay to the north and Argentina to the south. The Rio de la Plata is the widest river in the world, with a total area of about 13,500 square miles (34,964 km²) and a drainage of about 1,600,000 square miles (4,144,000 km²), which represents about one-fourth of the surface water of the continent.

ITAIPU DAM

The Itaipu Dam is located on the Alto Paraná River some 7.5 miles (12 km) north of Iguaçu Falls. The dam is 643 feet (196 m) high and 4.9 miles (8 km) long. The *power plant*, a building .9 mile (1.5 km) long that houses the equipment that converts water to electricity, is home to 18 massive turbine generators. The reservoir, which covers more than 700 square miles (1,812 km²), extends for 120 miles (193 km). Thanks to Iguaçu Falls, the Itaipu Dam produces enough electricity to supply the whole of southern Brazil and much of Rio de Janeiro, São Paulo, and Minas Gerais. Though the building of the dam has provided the benefits of electricity, clearing the forest in the area during construction has resulted in rapid runoff, large amounts of silt in the river, and bigger fluctuations in air temperature.

One of the largest single power stations in the world, the Itaipu Dam was built by Brazil and Paraguay. Construction began in 1975, and the 12,600-megawatt dam commenced operation in 1984. Paraguay, which does not need all the electricity generated for its use, sells part of its share to Brazil. Due to construction of the dam, the neighboring Brazilian city of Foz do Iguaçu has undergone a population and economic boom, and the city serves as the central tourist spot for visitors to Iguaçu Falls.

THE GUARANI AQUIFER

Underneath all that water flowing from Iguaçu Falls is more water. The Guarani Aquifer is the sixth-largest underground reservoir of water in the world. The aquifer extends more than 620,000 square miles (1,605,792 km²) from the Paraná Basin—located in Brazil, Paraguay, and Uruguay—to the Chaco Basin in Argentina.

Formed of layers of sand, the Guarani Aquifer developed during the Mesozoic Era, between 200 and 132 million years ago. Today it covers an area equal to that of England, France, and Spain combined. Ranging from 164 to 4,921 feet (50 to 1,500 m) deep, the Guarani Aquifer contains almost 10 trillion gallons (about 37 trillion L) of water and supplies some 15 million people in the region with freshwater. Scientists say that enough water is available to sustain 360 million people, but exploitation and pollution from garbage dumping, gasoline stations, and construction of cemeteries represent threats to the aquifer.

The nations that benefit from the supply of water are working together to protect the natural resource. The Guarani Aquifer Environmental Protection and Sustainable Development Plan, launched in 2003, is expected to cost $26.7 million. The World Bank, the Dutch and German governments, the International Body for Atomic Energy, and the Organization of American States will pay the tab for the project, which is expected to be completed in 2007.

The Guarani Aquifer stretches across 620,000 square miles (1,605,792 km²) in four South American countries.

EUROPEAN PRESENCE

Álvar Núñez Cabeza de Vaca was the first European to see Iguaçu Falls. Born in 1490 in Extremadura, Spain, he grew up to be an explorer. In 1528, he took part in an expedition that reached what is now Tampa Bay, Florida. One of only four members of the expedition who survived, he lived for eight years in the Gulf region of what is now Texas. Most likely, Cabeza de Vaca's explorations inspired Hernando de Soto and Francisco Vázquez de Coronado to explore North America.

Cabeza de Vaca arrived at Iguaçu Falls in 1541, during his search for a connection between the Brazilian coast and the Río de la Plata. At the falls, he attempted to change the name of the site to Santa María Falls, but Iguaçu, the name favored by the Guarani, prevailed. Cabeza de Vaca died in 1560, in Seville, Spain.

In 1609, Jesuit missionaries arrived in the area. They set up their first mission in Guaira, on the border of Paraguay, some 80 miles (130 km) north of Iguaçu Falls. The missionaries encouraged the original residents to weave their own clothing and dress like Europeans. They also raised cattle and built their own churches. Bandits from São Paulo, Brazil, invaded the mission in 1627, looking to capture slaves. The natives scattered into Paraguay, Argentina, and Brazil. Father Jose de Anchieta, a Jesuit working in São Paulo, spoke out against slavery, an opinion that was not appreciated at the time.

The Jesuits in the area continued to build schools and missions, and the natives formed their villages nearby, eager for the protection of the clergy. In 1755, Portugal freed all the natives from slavery, but the mandate had little effect. One year later, Portugal expelled the Jesuits from the missions in southern Brazil and Paraguay, installing directors willing to make profits from the forced labor of the native population. The Jesuits—and, apparently, the Portuguese—forgot all about Iguaçu Falls until a Brazilian expedition, dispatched by the president of Paraguay, arrived in 1863 to explore the area.

The Jesuits called the area where they settled the *Misiones*, or the Missions, now a province that covers 11,506 square miles (29,800 km²) on the Paraná Plateau. The terrain is rough, primarily rain forest and numerous canyons and rivers. Misiones was claimed by Argentina after years of dispute with Paraguay and Brazil, which resulted in the Paraguayan War of 1864–70. In 1882, the area received territorial status and acquired its capital, Posadas, from Corrientes province. Beginning in the 1880s, assorted ethnic groups—including Poles, Ukrainians, Japanese, Brazilians, German Brazilians, and Germans—settled the land. The territory gained provincial status in 1953, and today about 1 million people live in Misiones. Paraguayan tea, called maté, is the principal product of the area, which is also known for lumber and cassava. Wood processing is another important industry in the province.

IN THE FIELD: TRACKING PREDATORS IN THE PARK

From 1990 through 1999, biologist Dr. Peter Crawshaw directed The Carnivore Project in Iguaçu National Park, a study designed to monitor 10 species of land predators. The study was funded as part of Pro-Carnivores, a nonprofit organization based in São Paulo, Brazil. Crawshaw and his team of researchers placed radio-transmitter collars on more than 70 animals, including jaguars, pumas, jaguatiricas (small, pantherlike cats), ferrets, coatis, raccoons, and bush dogs.

Team members carefully captured, weighed, and measured each animal. Researchers then analyzed the condition of each animal's coat, calculated the age of the animal, took blood samples, and noted identifying characteristics. Tracking signals from the radio-transmitter collars, the scientists were able to verify the animals' movements and determine whether individual animals were on the move or resting at any one time.

Scientists were particularly interested in the jaguars, a highly endangered species. Iguaçu National Park is large enough to comfortably house about 170 jaguars, though at the time only about 50 of the cats were thought to be in the area. During the study, a large number of the collared animals were found shot, leading Crawshaw to suggest that jaguars could disappear entirely from the park by 2006. The panther population was also deemed to be at risk. To avoid further depletion of the cat population, the researchers recommended increased surveillance of the park and an aggressive education program for ranchers and hunters living in the area.

In 1999, the project was halted due to lack of funding. Currently, Crawshaw is seeking funding to support a national center of expertise on predators in Brazil, particularly the big cats, with a focus on resolving conflicts between humans and carnivores. Crawshaw notes that the center would "coordinate and act as a catalyst" for field studies, reintroduction and translocation projects, education programs, fund-raising, compensation schemes, and data collection on carnivores.

THREE CITIES, TWO BRIDGES

Tourism is the primary focus of three cities that benefit economically from the presence of Iguaçu Falls. The towns are connected literally as well. The Ponte da Fraternidade (Fraternity Bridge) connects Puerto Iguazu in the Argentinian province of Misiones to the Brazilian city of Foz do Iguaçu, and the Ponte da Amizade (Friendship Bridge) connects that city with Cuidad del Este, Paraguay.

Puerto Iguazu in Argentina is the smallest of the three cities, with a population of about 30,000. Foz do Iguaçu (which translates as Iguaçu Falls), in Brazil, has a population of 270,000, including many Africans, Arabs, Chinese, Germans, Italians, Lebanese, Paraguayans, Portuguese, and Ukrainians. Ciudad del Este, in Paraguay, is that country's second-largest city, with a population of about 240,000. The city has the second-largest Chinese colony of immigrants in Brazil and the third-largest Arab immigrant population. Ciudad del Este also has a large Asian population.

Considerable contrast exists between two of the towns. Foz do Iguaçu is pristine, something of a nature park that serves as a gateway to the falls. Ciudad del Este is a bustling town characterized by commercialism, a duty-free town known for cheap prices on every sort of merchandise. Thousands of shops fill the city with everything from electronic devices and pharmaceuticals to popular footwear and cheap plastic toys. In many populous neighborhoods, rotting food, plastic bags, and packing materials spill from the sidewalks into the streets, and daily traffic jams produce a thick odor of exhaust throughout the city that mingles with the stench of garbage.

Because of the proximity of the three towns to Iguaçu Falls, ecological threats to the rain forest are not uncommon. Current threats include fires, poaching of game and salmon, and the illegal felling of palm trees to collect palm hearts. The future of the area depends a great deal on the management of continued development of the three cities that benefit economically from the waterfall. Unaware of the battles raging around it, Iguaçu Falls roars on.

8

Multnomah Falls
North America

Some waterfalls are hidden from view and difficult to reach, but Multnomah Falls crashes down Larch Mountain in plain view of drivers traveling on the Historic Columbia River Highway through the Columbia River Gorge. A five-minute walk from a parking lot next to the highway leads to the base of the waterfall, one of the five tallest in the continental United States. Located about 30 miles (48 km) east of Portland, Multnomah Falls is also the highest waterfall in Oregon, a state that boasts hundreds of falls.

The two tiers of Multnomah Falls have a combined height of 620 feet (190 m). The upper portion measures 542 feet (165 m), and the lower falls is 69 feet (21 m). Multnomah Falls occurs on Multnomah Creek, a rock-filled waterway that meanders around Larch Mountain, drawing water from an underground spring, melting snow, and seasonal rains. Some six to eight miles (9 to 12 km) long, the creek boasts several stretches of rapids and numerous smaller falls before making the dramatic plunge. At the bottom of the waterfall, Multnomah Creek travels about a half mile (.8 km) to the Columbia River.

Multnomah Falls flows year-round, with the maximum volume during winter and spring. (Official records of volume do not exist.) The climate in the Columbia River Gorge is volatile, with occasional high winds and heavy rain. Rainfall varies by as much as 40 inches (101 cm) from one end of the gorge to the other. In the area of Multnomah Falls, the climate is moderate, with dry summers and the temperature averaging about 85°F (29°C). Most winters are mild, but, occasionally, arctic blasts shoot through the gorge in the form of an ice storm, known locally a "silver thaw." When that happens, Multnomah Falls freezes into complex ice formations, which hang from the side of Larch Mountain.

The name of the waterfall comes from the Multnomah, a tribe of Chinookan people who lived in the Portland area and in the Columbia River Gorge in the early 19th century. *Multnomah* translates as "down river." Tribal villages were located on both sides of the Columbia River. In 1806, the Multnomah tribe consisted of about 800 individuals. Within 30 years, the tribe was extinct. Some historians have used the term

During harsh winters, part of Multnomah Falls sometimes freezes into elegant ice formations. *(Peter Marbach Photography)*

Multnomah in a broader sense to include all the tribes that lived on or near the lower Willamette River in Oregon.

Like all waterfalls, Multnomah Falls changes all the time due to the force of the flowing water that erodes the rock face a bit every day. Sometimes the changes are more dramatic. On September 4, 1995, a 400-ton (362–metric ton) boulder broke away from the upper tier of the waterfall and crashed down 225 feet (69 m) into the upper plunge pool. The resulting splash rose up 70 feet (21 m), and bits of sharp gravel rained down on a wedding party standing on the pedestrian bridge above the lower falls. No one was seriously injured.

At the base of the falls is a lodge built of stones from the Columbia River Gorge that serves as a visitors' center, gift shop, and restaurant. The Oregon-Washington Railroad and Navigation Company donated the land for the lodge, which was completed in 1925, and it now is on the National Register of Historic Places.

THE MAN WHO OWNED MULTNOMAH FALLS

Simon Benson, a Norwegian-born logger and lumber baron, once owned Multnomah Falls. In the early 1900s, he purchased a 400-acre (161-ha) tract of land in the Columbia River Gorge that included Wahkeena Falls and Multnomah Falls. He later deeded the land to the city of Portland for a public park. The property was transferred to the USDA Forest Service in 1943 and divided into the Wahkeena Falls Recreation Area, Benson State Park, and the Multnomah Falls Recreation Area.

Benson was the kind of businessman who believed in sharing his wealth. He often was quoted as saying, "No one has the right to die and not leave something to the public and for the public good."

Born Simon Iverson on October 2, 1852, Benson was one of seven children. In 1867, the family came to New York. They moved to Black River Falls, Wisconsin, and there they changed the family name to Benson. Just 16 when he arrived in the United States, Simon Benson went to work as a farmhand. He later worked in logging camps and sawmills. He opened a general store at the age of 24 but lost everything three years later when the store was destroyed by fire. In 1880, Benson moved with his wife and child to Portland, Oregon. He went into the timber business, and over time he introduced a number of changes to the logging industry and became a wealthy man.

Benson built hotels—first in Portland and then near the Hood River—and was a member of a group of businessmen who encouraged the building of the Columbia River Highway. Benson helped fund the construction of a school in Portland, and he paid for 20 bronze drinking fountains placed throughout the city, some of which are still in use today. In 1914, Benson paid to replace a log bridge with a reinforced concrete pedestrian bridge over lower Multnomah Falls, shown in the lower color insert on page C-6. Named for Benson, the bridge spans the falls at the base of the first tier, providing a closer view of the power of water and a taste of the spray.

In the early 1920s, Benson retired to southern California, where he soon began to buy and develop land and to manage business properties. He died in Los Angeles on August 5, 1942. Benson is buried in Riverview Cemetery in Portland.

COLUMBIA RIVER

The largest river that flows into the Pacific Ocean from North America, the Columbia River makes its way some 1,240 miles (1,995 km) from its source in Columbia Lake in British Columbia to the Pacific Ocean north of Astoria, Oregon. The river's course is northwesterly for the first 190 miles (305 km), and it then shifts to flow south for 270 miles (434 km). After traveling some 500 miles (804 km) through Canada—much of that along the Canadian Rocky Mountains—the Columbia River enters northeastern Washington, where it carves out a sweeping curve known as the Big Bend, an area known for its steep-walled ravines. Just after its confluence with the Snake River, the Columbia heads west for 300 miles (482 km), forming the boundary between Oregon and Washington before spilling into the Pacific Ocean.

The Columbia River drains some 258,000 square miles (668,216 km^2), much of it in the United States. Only the Mississippi, St. Lawrence, and Mackenzie Rivers exceed the Columbia in discharge in North America. The Kootenay, Snake, Pend Oreille, Spokane, Okanogan, Yakima, Cowlitz, and Willamette Rivers are tributaries of the Columbia. The river runs fastest in spring and early summer, and the level drops in autumn and winter. One of the world's greatest sources of hydroelectric power, the Columbia and its tributaries represent one-third of the potential hydropower of the United States.

The climate of the Columbia River basin varies widely. The Rocky Mountains keep at bay most of the severe winter storms that affect the land to the east, and the Cascade Range on the west side of the basin blocks out moist air from the Pacific Ocean. West of the Cascades, winters are rainy and summers are cool and dry. East of the Cascades, summers tend to be hot and dry and winters moderate, with occasional snow or rain. Elevation influences temperature and precipitation. In the central basin, the average temperature in January ranges from 25° to 30°F (−4° to −1°C). In July the average temperature ranges from 70° to 75°F (21° to 24°C), but the temperature can rise as high as 85° to 95°F (29° to 35°C). The average annual rainfall ranges from less than eight inches (20 cm) at the lowest elevations to about 15 inches (38 cm) in the foothills and 40 inches (101 cm) high in the mountains.

Sagebrush and other shrubs, along with willow and black cottonwood trees, grow in the lower regions of the Columbia River basin. Ponderosa pine, fir trees, larch trees, and other pines are found at higher elevations. Douglas fir, hemlock, and western red cedar trees grow west of the Cascade Range. Once-abundant animal life—including black bear, elk, and mule deer—has suffered greatly as a result of the human population. Bald eagles and peregrine falcons in the area are considered threatened and endangered species, respectively, and beaver populations are drastically reduced.

In 1883, some 21,500 tons (19,504 metric tons) of salmon were caught in the Columbia River. The catch is about 10 percent of that today. Though some organizations and agencies have attempted to increase the size of the annual salmon run, experts say the fish population will likely continue to decrease, for several reasons. Among them are flooding, dams and other power-generating equipment on the river, and changes in the river's natural current, which once guided spawning salmon.

The Columbia River got its name from a ship owned by Robert Gray, a trader from Boston who sailed up the river in 1792. Native Americans lived in the Columbia River basin for several thousand years before Gray made the journey, and Spanish explorers recorded seeing the mouth of the river in 1775. The Lewis and Clark expedition spent the winter of 1805 and 1806 at Fort Clatsop near Astoria. Fort Walla Walla was built on the river in 1818, and Fort Vancouver was built in 1825. By 1887, the coming of the railroad had ended the Columbia River's reign as a major transportation artery, but the river remains the only inland waterway route to the Pacific Ocean in North America.

BONNEVILLE LOCK AND DAM

Not far from Multnomah Falls on the Columbia River is the Bonneville Lock and Dam, which is made up of several structures that span the river between Oregon and Washington. Built and managed by the Army Corps of Engineers, the *power plant* at the dam houses equipment that converts water to electrical power, and the dam aids navigation of the river.

The Corps began construction of the lock, a power plant, and a spillway in 1933 and finished in 1937. Before the river was dammed at the site, a set of locks built in 1896 moved ships around the Cascade Rapids, located several miles upstream from Bonneville. Lake Bonneville, the 48-mile (77-km)-long reservoir that formed behind the new dam, submerged the old lock structure.

A second powerhouse was built between 1974 and 1981. During construction, the river channel was widened on the Washington side. The combined electrical output of the two powerhouses at Bonneville Lock and Dam is now over 1 million kilowatts. A new lock was completed on the Oregon side in 1993.

The Bonneville Lock and Dam is named for Army Captain Benjamin Bonneville, an early explorer who charted much of the Oregon Trail. The dam has also been connected with legendary folk singer Woody Guthrie, who made mention of it in his song "Roll On, Columbia." In 1941, Guthrie worked for one month for the U.S. Department of the Interior, writing 26 songs about the Columbia River and the dams being built along it.

THE COLUMBIA RIVER GORGE

Carved by the Columbia River through the Cascade Range, the Columbia River Gorge (as seen in the upper color insert on page C-7) is the only sea-level passage through the Cascade Mountains. The gorge is 80 miles (128 km) long, with sheer rock walls that rise as high as 4,000 feet (1,219 m). The north canyon walls are in Washington, and the south canyon walls are in Oregon. Conifer trees, big-leaf maple, cottonwood, Oregon ash, and vine maple line the western side of the gorge, while Oregon white oak and ponderosa pine flourish on the eastern side. On November 17, 1986, Congress designated the Columbia River Gorge the nation's first National Scenic Area.

A series of volcanic eruptions that resulted in massive flows of *basalt*, sometimes known as basalt floods, helped determine the course of the Columbia River while it carved the gorge. Dark in color, fine-grained, and heavy, basalt is the most common form of *lava*, also known as *magma*. Over 17 million year ago, great quantities of basalt lava oozed from cracks in the Earth's surface, building layers of basalt up to 16,404 feet (5,000 m) thick.

The basalt lava was relatively fluid, and this inhibited the formation of volcano cones where the magma broke through the Earth's crust. Instead the lava flows covered large areas of land. Over time, some 300 individual basalt floods occurred, covering 101,904 square miles (263,930 km²) in what is now northeast Oregon, southwest Washington, and western Idaho. As the basalt floods solidified, *joints* occurred in the rocks. Joints are similar to *faults*, which are rock fractures where land has been significantly displaced. Unlike faults, joints occur with tiny movements of rock on either side of the break. As basalt cools, the lava shrinks between 5 to 10 percent as it hardens, and this causes joints to form. Some of the rock that resulted from the basalt floods is exposed along the cliffs of the Columbia River Gorge, and different patterns of joints are visible.

Some of the basalt floods permanently altered the path of the Columbia River, gradually pushing the river north. The oldest channel of the Columbia River was altered some 15.4 million years ago by a basalt flow that destroyed drainage systems throughout most of the Columbia Plateau. A basalt flow that occurred 14.5 million years ago overwhelmed the channel and forced the river northward. Some 12 million years ago, the river's channel was moved once more. Six to 2 million years ago, basalt floods forced the river north to its former canyon. The present-day Columbia River Gorge began to form 2 million years ago as the Cascade Range experienced *uplift*, or a gradual rise, as a result of the shifting earth.

Floods of another sort also played a role in the formation of the Columbia River Gorge. During the Ice Age (some 12,000 to 19,000 years ago), glaciers in western Montana advanced and retreated as many as 40 times. Thick rivers of ice repeatedly pressed forward, pushing aside whatever lay in the path, and then pulled back. As the climate grew milder, the glaciers melted and sent torrents of water into the areas previously carved out by ice. These floods—equal to 10 times the combined flow of the rivers of the world—thundered across Idaho, Washington, and Oregon, scouring the walls of canyons with boulders and rocky debris carried by the racing water and widening what is now known as the Columbia River Gorge.

J. Harlen Bretz, a geologist, first described the flood phenomenon in the early 1920s. His hypothesis is currently known as the Bretz Floods or the Ice Age Floods. The National Park Service recently completed a report on the Bretz Floods, which they have submitted to Congress for designation as the "Ice Age Floods National Geologic Trail." The designation is pending.

ADDITIONAL WATERFALLS

The Columbia River Gorge is home to at least 75 waterfalls. Most of them are on the Oregon side of the gorge, but a few are in Washington. The largest and most dramatic waterfalls are on the Oregon side because landslides have repeatedly eroded the slope on the Washington side, where the walls of the gorge tilt slightly southward. The waterfalls described here are all on the Oregon side.

Wahkeena Falls, located a half mile (.8 km) west of Multnomah Falls, plunges 242 feet (73 m) along Wahkeena Creek. *Wahkeena* is a word from the Yakama tribe that means "most beautiful." Triple Falls, some 2.5 miles (4 km) east of Multnomah Falls on Oneonta Creek, consists of three separate falls ranging from 100 to 135 feet (30 to 41 m) high. Nearby, along Horsetail Creek, is Horsetail Falls, which is 176 feet (53 m) high.

Other falls in the area include Latourell and Upper Latourell, both on Larch Mountain. Latourell Falls drops 249 feet (75 m) and Upper Latourell Falls ranges from 75 to 100 feet (22 to 30 m) high, depending on the season. Both falls occur on Latourell Creek, named for Joseph Latourell, an early settler in the Columbia River Gorge.

Shepperds Dell Falls at Shepperds Dell State Park is a two-tiered waterfall, with one drop ranging from 35 to 50 feet (9 to 15 m) and one from 40 to 60 feet (12 to 18 m). Bridal Veil Falls, from the creek of the same name, also has two tiers; one between 60 and 100 feet (18 and 30 m) high and one ranging from 40 to 60 feet (12 to 18 m) high. Fairy Falls, along Wahkeena Creek, is broader at the bottom than the top. The drop is 20 to 30 feet (6 to 9 m) high.

Farther east of Multnomah Falls, in the Tanner Creek and Eagle Creek area, is Wahclella Falls with its two roaring tiers, one some 70 feet (21 m) high and one 25 feet (7 m) high. Metlako Falls, named for an Indian goddess of salmon, drops between 100 and 150 feet (30 and 45 m). Punch Bowl Falls, which pours out of a narrow opening into a broad pool, ranges from 10 to 15 feet (3 to 4.5 m) high.

EARLY SETTLERS

People have lived in the Columbia River Gorge for over 31,000 years. Archaeological digs have revealed evidence of the Folsom and Marmes people, who crossed the Great Continental Divide from Asia, and humans have occupied Five Mile Rapids for more than 10,000 years. Others living on the banks of the Columbia River included the ancestors of today's Yakama, Warm Springs, Umatilla, and Nez Perce tribes. Native Americans from other areas in North America also traveled to the Columbia River Gorge, to trade for dried, smoked salmon.

In the early 1800s, explorers and fur traders—including Meriwether Lewis and William Clark—ventured into the gorge. David Douglas, a botanist, and John Townsend, an ornithologist, also came to the area. Still others came to explore, to document the geology of the land, and to study geography, plants, and animals. In 1843, some 900 people traveled the 2,000-mile (3,218-km) Oregon Trail to reach the Willamette Valley. By 1849 Oregon was home to some 11,500 pioneers.

THE CASCADE RANGE

Named for the dramatic waterfalls along the Columbia River Gorge—Multnomah Falls among them—the Cascade Mountains boast about two dozen prominent peaks. The Cascades stretch for more than 700 miles (1,100 km) from Lassen Peak, located in northern California, north through Oregon and Washington to the Fraser River in southern British Columbia, Canada. The range lies 100 to 150 miles (160 to 240 km) inland from the Pacific Ocean and varies in width from 50 to 120 miles (80 to 193 km). All but the highest peaks above the timberline are heavily wooded, and most of the mountains are located in conservation areas and national forests. North of the Cascade Mountains, the Coast Mountains of British Columbia continue the range, and the Sierra Nevada extends the chain to the south.

The Cascade Range is divided into the old and the new Cascades. The west side is known as the old Cascades (Western Cascade Group), while the east side is known as the new Cascades (High Cascade Group). The Cascades were formed 40 to 5 million years ago through movement beneath the Earth's crust.

A TRIBAL TALE

Members of the Wasco Tribe tell a tale of how Multnomah Falls was formed. One condensed version of the tale is as follows:

"Long, long ago, when the world was young and people had not come out yet, the animals and the birds were the people of this country. Coyote was the most powerful of the animal people, for he had been given special power by the Spirit Chief.

"Coyote made one of his frequent trips along Great River [Columbia River]. He stopped when he came to the place where the water flowed under the Great Bridge that joined the mountains on one side of the river with the mountains on the other side. There he changed himself into a handsome young hunter. When traveling up the river the last time, he had seen a beautiful girl in a village not far from the bridge. He made up his mind that he would ask the girl's father if he might have her for his wife. The girl's father was a chief. When the handsome young man went to the chief's lodge, he carried with him a choice gift for the father in return for his daughter.

"The gift was pleasing in the father's eyes, but he wanted his daughter to be pleased. 'She is my only daughter,' the chief said to the young hunter. 'And she is very dear to my heart. I shall not be like other fathers and trade her for a pile of furs. You will have to win the heart of my daughter, for I want her to be happy.' So Coyote came to the chief's lodge every day, bringing with him some small gift that he thought would please the girl. But he never seemed to bring the right thing. She would shyly accept his gift and the run away to the place where the women sat in the sun doing their work with deerskins or to the place where the children were playing games.

"Every day Coyote became more eager to win the beautiful girl. He asked the chief what gift he could bring that would win her heart. The chief answered, 'Why don't you ask my daughter? Ask her today what gift will make her heart the happiest of all hearts.'

"Coyote stepped up to her and asked, 'Oh, beautiful one, what does your heart want most of all? I will get for you anything that you name.' She answered, 'I want a pool where I may bathe every day hidden from all eyes that might see.'

"Coyote turned to her father. 'It is well. In seven suns I will come for you and your daughter. I will take you to the pool she asked for. The pool will be for her alone.' For seven suns Coyote worked to build the pool. First he cut a great gash in the hills on the south side of Great River. Then he lined that gash with trees and shrubs and ferns to the very top of a high wall that looked toward the river.

"Then he went to the bottom of the rock wall and slanted it back a long way, far enough to hollow out a wide pool. He climbed up the wall again and went far back into the hills. There he made a stream come out of the earth, and he sent it down the big gash he had made, to fall over the slanting rock wall. From the edge of that wall the water dropped with spray and mist. And so the water made, at the bottom, a big screen that hid the pool from all eyes.

"When he had finished his work, Coyote went to the village to invite the chief and his daughter to see what he had made. When they had admired the new waterfall, he showed them the pool that lay behind it and the spray. The girl looked with smiling eyes, and Coyote could see that at last he had won her heart."

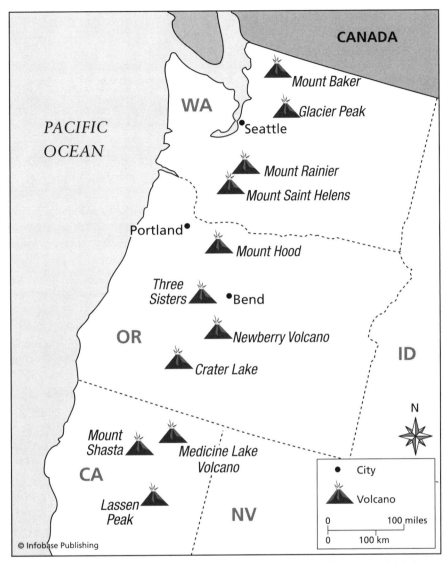

A line of primarily dormant volcanoes stretches along the Cascade Range, which forms a barrier between east and west from Washington south to northern California.

Many peaks in the Cascade Mountains exceed 10,000 feet (3,000 m). Mount Rainier, in Washington, stands at 14,410 feet (4,392 m) and is the highest mountain in the range. The main cone of the volcano was formed starting 730,000 years ago. Though the most recent eruption was about 2,200 years ago, Mount Rainier is considered the most dangerous volcano in the Cascades because the steep mountain is covered in large amounts of ice and snow and sits near a large population center. The peak is known for avalanches of debris. Mount Hood, in Oregon, is 11,235 feet (3,424 m) high and the tallest peak in Oregon. The main cone of Mount Hood formed about 500,000 years ago, and the volcano has had four eruptive periods in the last 15,000 years. Most recently—some 250 to 180 years ago—lava domes collapsed and fresh flows buried the southwest flank of the mountain.

Most of the mountains in the Cascade Range are dormant volcanoes, though Lassen Peak experienced an eruptive period from 1914 through 1917. Mount Baker emitted heavy steam in 1975. More recently, Mount St. Helens erupted on May 18, 1980. The north face of the mountain collapsed in a massive rock debris avalanche, destroying nearly 230 square miles (595 km²) of forest. A mushroom-shaped column of ash rose high in the sky and drifted downwind, turning day into night as dark, gray ash fell over eastern Washington and beyond. The eruption lasted nine hours and is considered the most destructive volcanic eruption in the history of the United States.

BEACON ROCK

Seven miles east of Multnomah Falls, on the Washington side of the Columbia River Gorge, is Beacon Rock, an 848-foot (258-m)-high rock that towers above the Columbia River. Geologists believe that Beacon Rock, located in Beacon Rock State Park, may be the exposed *volcanic plug*, or core, of an ancient mountain that was part of a range that preceded the Cascades some 9 million years ago. A volcanic plug is a mass of volcanic rock that solidifies when lava hardens in the vent of a volcano. The rock that makes up the plug may be so hard that when the rest of the volcano becomes extinct and starts to erode away during floods or shifts in the land, the plug remains in place. Ship Rock, in New Mexico, the remnant of an explosive volcanic eruption that occurred around 30 million years ago, is another example of a volcanic plug, also known as a volcanic neck. Part of an elongated rock formation, Ship Rock stands 1,968 feet (600 m) high and measures 1,640 feet (500 m) in diameter.

For hundreds of years, Beacon Rock served as a landmark for river travelers. Native Americans knew that the rock marked the last of the rapids on the Columbia River and the beginning of tidal influence from the Pacific Ocean, some 150 miles (214 km) away. Explorers Lewis and Clark are said to be the first white men to see Beacon Rock, and they named it during their expedition to the Pacific Ocean. The notation appears in a journal entry dated October 31, 1805.

In 1811, Alexander Ross of the John Jacob Astor expedition called the rock "Inoshoack Castle." For the next 105 years, the rock was known as Castle Rock. In 1916, the U.S. Board of Geographic Names restored the name to Beacon Rock.

Around 1900, the Army Corps of Engineers decided to blow up Beacon Rock. Railroad officials, concerned that rocks would fall on and damage newly laid tracks, opposed the plan, and the demolition was canceled. In 1915 a businessman named Henry Biddle bought Beacon Rock and built a trail to its summit. The project cost $15,000. Biddle instructed his family that they were to sell Beacon Rock to the state of Washington for $1 when he died, with the provision that the land was to be preserved as a public park.

One version of the story notes that after Biddle died in 1925, his bereaved family approached state officials, who declined to promise to use the land as a park. The Biddle family then contacted officials in Oregon. Political leaders in Washington quickly paid the dollar and made the promise. Today a three-quarter-mile (1-km) trail to the top of Beacon Rock switches back 52 times and crosses 22 wooden bridges. The Hamilton Mountain Trail, also located in Beacon Rock State Park, leads to Hardy Falls, one of the few waterfalls on the Washington side of the Columbia River Gorge. Hardy Falls occurs on Hardy Creek and measures between 80 and 120 feet (24 and 36 m) high, depending on the season.

IN THE FIELD: AIR QUALITY IN THE COLUMBIA RIVER GORGE

In 2001, air-quality agencies in Washington and Oregon announced that they were seeking public comments on a plan to create a clean-air strategy for the Columbia River Gorge National Scenic Area. The Columbia River Gorge Commission requested that the plan be developed "to protect and enhance air quality, and foster economic development in the gorge." The request developed as a result of haze rated as "noticeable" in the area 90 percent of the time. The researchers who reported the haze also found signs that air pollution was affecting vegetation.

The draft plan was developed by the Washington Department of Ecology, the Oregon Department of Environmental Quality (DEQ), and the Southwest Clean Air Agency (SWCAA), with assistance from the U.S. Forest Service, the six scenic area counties, and other interested parties. The plan outlined research into air quality in the gorge and described a strategy-development process that relied heavily on public participation.

In August 2005, the DEQ and SWCAA presented a project status report to the Columbia River Gorge Commission. They reported that the Air Quality Study was "on track, on schedule, and on budget," and researchers promised to produce two key reports on air quality in 2006 and early 2007.

The U.S. Forest Service also reported initiation of a study on potential impacts from air pollution on soil, flora, and archaeological resources and noted incidents of "high acid deposition" at the east end of the gorge.

That information will be used to develop air-quality goals and emission reduction strategies for the gorge.

THE FUTURE OF COLUMBIA RIVER GORGE

In the fall 2005 *Oregon Historical Quarterly*, Jim R. O'Connor writes that "Travelers retracing Lewis and Clark's journey to the Pacific over the past two hundred years have witnessed tremendous change to the Columbia River Gorge and its primary feature, the Columbia River. Dams, reservoirs, timber harvest, altered fisheries, transportation infrastructure, and growth and shrinkage of communities have transformed the river and valley." And yet, O'Connor notes, though human-caused changes have been profound, "the geologic history of immense floods, landslides, and volcanic eruptions that occurred before their journey had equally, if not more, acute effects on landscapes and societies of the gorge."

The Columbia River remains a major transportation route through the Cascade Mountains as barges carry grain, livestock, lumber, fruit and vegetables grown and processed in the Columbia River basin. The area also serves as an important recreation area, drawing more than 2.5 million visitors each year, many of them eager to take advantage of the easy access to the tallest waterfall in the gorge—Multnomah Falls.

9

Jog Falls

Asia

"What have you seen in life, if you haven't seen the Jog Falls?" So goes a folk song, especially beloved by children, about the tallest waterfall in India. Jog Falls, a spectacular show of force during monsoon season, is located in mountains on the border between the districts of Shimoga and North Kanara in the state of Karnataka in the southwestern part of the country. Some know the waterfall as Gersoppa, the name of a village 11 miles (18 km) from the bottom of the falls, but Jog Falls is by far the more widely used name.

Surrounded by dense forests and wooded mountains, Jog Falls consists of four distinct cascades of water that stretch across 1,550 feet (472 m) of rock wall, as shown in the lower color insert on page C-7. The streams are known locally as Raja, Rani, Roarer, and Rocket. Raja, which means "king," is the tallest of the four, plummeting 830 feet (253 m). The mist-covered pool at the base of Raja is 132 feet (40 m) deep. Rani, a Hindi word for "queen," winds and twists in a manner resembling the movements of a female dancer. The cascade is also known as *La Dame Blanche*, or "The white lady." Roarer splashes out from a mass of rocks. Rocket sends a large volume of water gushing at high speed from a small opening.

The average volume of Jog Falls has been reported at 40,297 gallons (152,540 L) per second during the late summer months, when the floodgates of a nearby dam are opened. During periods of *monsoons*, wind patterns that result in heavy rain roughly from June through November, the highest-recorded volume at Jog Falls has reached 897,662 gallons (3,398,020 L) per second, a dramatic blast of water by any standard. Steps have been cut into the rock at the falls for adventurous visitors eager to feel the spray.

Like all waterfalls, Jog Falls is always changing, eroding, and cutting into the rock face of the cliff. Geologists suggest that to date, Jog Falls has receded some 13 miles (21 km) from its original location. Scientists also speculate that if the Sharavati River were to be diverted into a new

Much of the Sharavati River's route winds through deep forests nurtured each year by the monsoon season. *(K. L. Kamat/Kamat's Potpourri)*

channel over the next several thousand years, a new waterfall as significant as Jog Falls could form.

THE SHARAVATI RIVER

Jog Falls is fed by the Sharavati River, a minor river that begins its journey at Ambuthirtha in mountains called the Western Ghats. The river flows 60 miles (95 km) northwest to Honavar, a town on the Arabian Sea. About 18 miles (29 km) upriver from its mouth, the Sharavati River widens to 230 feet (70 m), splits into four streams, and then drops, forming Jog Falls.

Much of the river's route is through deep forests nurtured by an average annual rainfall of 98 inches (2,500 mm). During monsoon season, as much as 299 inches (7,600 mm) may fall, swelling all the rivers and greening the valleys. Though the temperature can exceed 86°F (30°C) during April and May and drop to 32°F (0°C) in the higher hills in the winter, the mean temperature ranges between 68° and 75°F (20° and 24°C).

The Sharavati River initially flowed east along the surface of a plateau. The river then changed course, heading west, due to a phenomenon called *river capture*. River capture occurs when one stream erodes in such a way that it cuts off another stream, diminishing the flow of the captured stream when the "pirate" stream rises above the point of capture. The new course and the additional volume of water renew the stream, causing it to run faster and carve deeper gorges than before. Geologists say that the current drainage of the Sharavati River is a result of extensive erosion millions of years ago in the Western Ghats. The erosion led to the river capture, which caused the Sharavati to change course and flow to the Arabian Sea. That erosion has been so extensive that no one can say exactly where the Sharavati was originally captured and rerouted.

GNEISS AND GRANITE

Jog Falls is situated in a mountain range known as the Western Ghats. The mountains are made up primarily of gray *gneiss*, a coarse, high-grade metamorphic rock that was subjected to extreme heat and pressure during its formation some 3 to 4 million years ago. Some gneiss originates from granite, and some is derived from other, softer metamorphic rock. Gneiss is typically banded, made up of alternating layers of different minerals that occur perpendicular to the directions of pressure or that show the layering associated with the original sedimentary layers. Feldspar and quartz are among the minerals found in gneiss that form the lighter bands in the rock. Minerals such as mica, garnet, and graphite form the darker bands.

Schist, another metamorphic rock, is also found in the area. Often green in color, schist is softer than gneiss and has a tendency to split into layers. Unlike gneiss, schist is rarely banded but has a grainy, flaky appearance. Most schist, which occurs in wide belts, was originally composed of clay and mud.

Granite is also found in the Western Ghats. Granite is *intrusive igneous rock*, or rock that forms when *magma*, or molten rock, cools and hardens underground. Granite is coarse-grained, a composite of different mineral crystals or molten magma that cooled together below the surface of the Earth. Gneiss, schist, and granite all form different layers of the planet, as shown in the illustration on page 112.

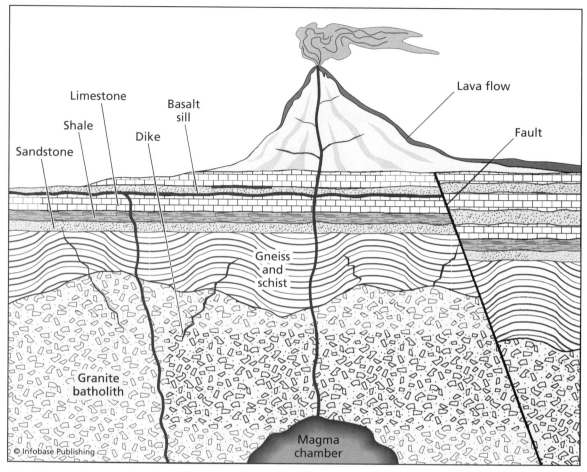

This diagram shows various layers of rock, including gneiss, schist, and granite, all found in the Western Ghats in India.

WESTERN GHATS

The Western Ghats—also known as the Sahyadri Mountains (the Sanskrit name)—cover a 99,000-square-mile (160,000-km²) area of forested land that stretches 994 miles (1,600 km) from the southern tip of the country to Gujarat in the north. Along the western coast, the mountains are some 18 to 31 miles (30 to 50 km) inland and are characterized by steep, dramatic cliffs. The average elevation of the mountains throughout the range is 3,937 feet (1,200 m). *Ghat* is a Hindi word for mountain pass, but for centuries, the word has been used for the mountain range itself. (Another meaning of the word *ghat* is a terraced riverbank where people come to bathe or do laundry.)

Across the continent, the Eastern Ghats, with an average elevation of 1,500 feet (457 m), reach down the Madras coast from the Orissa district south to Tinnevelly. In Ganjam and Vizagapatam, where the mountains are close to the Bay of Bengal, the peaks are higher, ranging from 4,000 feet (1,219 m) to 5,000 feet (1,524 m). The Eastern Ghats meet the Western Ghats at Cape Comorin, the southernmost tip of India.

The Western Ghats range is divided into three sections. Jog Falls is located in the middle section of the Western Ghats in the state of Karnataka (formerly Mysore), where the elevation ranges from 1,968 feet (600 m) to 2,952 feet (900 m). The southern section, primarily in the state of Kerala, has the highest ranges, including Anai Mudi, the highest peak in the Ghats, which boasts an elevation of 8,841 feet (2,695 m). A single forest in the southern district houses limestone pinnacles, slender spikes of rock found nowhere else in the Western Ghats, though they are common in many other forests in Southeast Asia. The northern section of the Western Ghats, located primarily in the state of Maharashtra, has an average elevation of 1,804 feet (550 m).

The formation of the Western Ghats took place during a period of volcanic activity that lasted some 120 to 130 million years. During that activity, the peninsula now known as India tilted to the east, causing some rivers to flow west. Today 27 major rivers in India flow west and 38 flow east. These drainage patterns, along with additional tectonic movement deep inside the Earth, have formed along faults and fractures in the Western Ghats, including steep drops such as that at Jog Falls.

Jog Falls is just one of several waterfalls in the Western Ghats. The Cauvery River feeds a double fall, also known as a twin fall, in the Mandya district. The twin falls, known as Gaganachukki and Bharachukki, are about .5 mile (1 km) apart. The Shimsha River also drops once in the same district. Two falls, Abbi and Irrupu, are in the Kodagu district.

In the Chikmagalur district, Hebbe Falls plunges some 500 feet (152 m) while Kallatti Falls drops 400 feet (121 m). Manikyandhara Falls is located near Baba Budangiri Dattatreya Peetha, a famous pilgrim center. The Mysore district is known for Chunchanakatte Falls. Uttar Kannada district is famous for its Unchalli (Lushington) Falls. Some 11 miles (19 km) away, Gokak Falls is known as "Mini Niagara" because of its broad spread.

DECCAN PLATEAU

The Western Ghats make up one edge of the triangular-shaped Deccan Plateau that comprises much of central and southern India. The Deccan Plateau, also known as the Deccan Traps, is one of the largest subcontinental outpourings of plateau *basalt* lavas. Basalt, the most common form of lava, is dark, fine-grained, and heavy. At one time, the Deccan Plateau covered more than 621,371 square miles (1,609,300 km²), with an average thickness of just over .5 mile (1 km). The area now extends about 250,000 square miles (647,497 km²), or roughly the size of Washington and Oregon combined. The basalt lava extends from the plateau up into the Western Ghats, where the soil is rich in iron and manganese, due to eroded particles of ancient metamorphic rock.

The basalt beds of the Deccan Plateau were formed at the end of the Cretaceous Period, some 65 million years ago, during a long period of volcanic activity. Molten lava flowed at the surface and solidified into a hard rocky layer with each eruption, forming a series of layers. By the time the volcanoes ceased to erupt, the basalt beds had formed a region of plateaus, one rich in minerals such as mica and iron ore. Diamonds, gold, and other metals are also found in the region.

LINGANMAKKI DAM

Just 3.5 miles (6 km) above Jog Falls on the Sharavati River sits the Linganmakki Dam, the main feeder reservoir for the Mahatma Gandhi Hydroelectric Power Plant. The dam rises 1,819 feet (554 m) above sea level. The *power plant*—the building that houses equipment that converts water into electricity—has been in operation since 1949 and generates some 1,200 megawatts, one of the largest hydroelectric stations in India. The reservoir and power plant provide drinking water and electrical power for millions of Indian citizens.

Legend has it that early in the 1900s, an engineer and statesman from Karnataka took one look at Jog Falls—which then flowed robustly all year—and said, "What a waste." His disdainful comment led to construction of the power plant. Originally named Krishna Rajendra Hydroelectric Project (after a former king of Mysore), the name of the power plant was later changed to honor Mahatma Gandhi, the internationally respected spiritual and political leader of India.

The reservoir and power plant considerably deplete the majesty of Jog Falls for much of the year. However, sometimes during the monsoon season, the floodgates of the dam are opened, and the waterfall runs full. In the *Deccan Herald*, a district newspaper, a writer lamented in April 2005 that "Jog Falls is today nonexistent" and that "in its place, there are dry rocks standing in sepulcherous silence." The writer continues, "Only Roarer seems to roar in disturbed and desperate voice, asking the madness to cease. Jog Falls has become a joke mankind seems to have played on nature, oblivious of the consequences."

SHIMOGA DISTRICT

Jog Falls is 62 miles (100 km) from the city of Shimoga, the administrative center of the district of the same name. The district covers 6,557 square miles (16,982 km²) and houses more than 1.6 million people. The word *Shimoga* is a derivative of the term *Shiva-Mukha*, which translates as "Face of Shiva." Shiva is one of the primary gods in the Hindu religion.

MEMORIES OF JOG FALLS

In the *Deccan Herald* newspaper on August 3, 2004, M. Bhaktavatsala writes of making the trip to Jog Falls as a young man. He recalls traveling by train from the city of Shimoga to Talaguppa, where the tracks end, and then proceeding by bullock cart or on foot. "One could of course drive all the way," he writes, "but then, those were fuel-scarce war years and the buses were coal fired. It was a terribly bumpy, dusty and extremely hot ride."

Bhaktavatsala writes that "animals abounded on the hill slopes" and in the forests along the way. "One got tired of looking at peacocks, wild dogs, jackals, slithering snakes and even bisons. You stopped to watch only when tigers majestically crossed the road or when you sighted leopards crouching on top of boulders. The sloth bear was a little less frequent, but no one was interested in it."

The approach to Jog Falls provided a perfect setting for viewing what the author calls a "great spectacle." He continues:

The sound of the eagerly sought after spectacle came long before the sight of it. It began like the prolonged rumbling of the monsoon clouds gradually intensifying into an all-pervading roar, at once unearthly and humbling. The ear-shattering din of the waters when one came closer was truly frightening. The spray thrown up by the fierce waters drenched you and the deep chasm separating you from the roaring waters seemed only a breath away. One stepped out of the car only to immediately retreat behind it.

There was Raja with yellow streaks in his bulging muscles, swelling with power. It jutted out as though the mountain had crumbled under its force and was going to swallow one at any moment. Next to Raja, Rani was a subdued poem. It hugged each crag while pouring down and in the middle, where the waist would be, it took a delicate turn, spewing wispy white feathery waters that seemed to take its graceful time in landing, so unlike the yellow-streaked warrior on the right who plunged down in one massive thrust. Roarer was a hound, a bulldog that snarled out a fierce mass of water from somewhere around the knee height of Raja and Rani. Rocket, of course, was a delight. It poured straight down and then suddenly spurted out clear of the rock into a vast spray of pure silver.

That, according to the author, was Jog Falls before 1950, before the construction of the Linganmakki Dam on the Sharavati River just above Jog Falls. Bhaktavatsala writes that today, the approach to Jog Falls is barren country and the "fall is now reduced to a trickle over rocks, viewed to the accompaniment of transistor music, blaring horns and a babble of human voices." He notes that "Jog is just water if you are scientifically inclined, otherwise it is pure mist-filled magic, at once ethereal and larger than life." Viewers that hold either opinion will find, he says, that "the waters are now tamed, subdued and made to serve the needs of civilization."

Known as "the bread basket" and "the rice bowl" of Karnataka, Shimoga is famous for its fertile soil and picturesque landscapes, including hills, valleys, rivers, forests, rice paddies, and, of course, waterfalls. The district is in a region where bamboo, teak, and rosewood grow. Among the wildlife present are elephants, gaurs (wild oxen), langur monkeys, and tigers.

Karnataka is primarily a rural and agrarian state. The eighth-largest state in India, Karnataka boasts a population of about 52.7 million people.

Kannada is the predominant language. The state covers 119,173 square miles (308,656 km²), or just over 5 percent of the total area of the country. The name Karnataka is from the Hindu word *karunadu*, which translates as "lofty land." Much of Karnataka lies on the Deccan Plateau, though the Western Ghats separate the narrow strip of coastal plains from the plateau. A hand ax from the Stone Age, recovered at the town of Lingasugur in Raichur district, is the earliest artifact found to date in Karnataka.

Bangalore, said to be the fastest-growing city in Asia, is the capital of Karnataka. The city is known as the telecommunications center of India and is home to many of the country's electronic and scientific industries. Bangalore is also known as a center for aeronautics, aircraft manufacturing, and machinery manufacturing.

KARNATAKA TODAY AND YESTERDAY

Karnataka is divided into four geographic regions: the Karnataka Coastal Region, the Northern Karnataka Plateau, the Central Karnataka Plateau, and the Southern Karnataka Plateau. Much of the state is known for its natural beauty, ranging from the 161-mile (260-km)-long coastline to the rolling hills of the Western Ghats to the forested plateau. Currently, Karnataka attracts the largest number of tourists in southern India. The state is also known for its coffee and tea plantations as well as its timber and minerals.

The two important river systems in Karnataka are the Krishna and the Cauvery, which both flow eastward to the Bay of Bengal. Among the Krishna River's tributaries are the Bhima, Ghataprabha, Malaprabha, Tungabhadra, and Vedavati. Tributaries of the Cauvery River include the Hemavati, Shimsha, Arkavati, Lakshmana Thirtha, and Kabini. Only a few small rivers—among them the Sharavati, Kalinadi, and Netravati—flow westward to the Arabian Sea.

Colorful dynasties ruled Karnataka in the early days of the area. Among those dynasties were the Mauryas, the Chalukyas, the Hoysalas, and the Vijayanagaras. In the seventh century, the Chalukyans built some of the earliest Hindu temples in India. The Hoysalas, who ruled from the 11th to the 13th century, built an additional 150 temples, each considered an artistic and architectural masterpiece. During the Vijayanagara Empire, scholarship and the fine arts flourished. Later dynasties enhanced the area's reputation for fine art and architecture.

In the 18th century, Hyder Ali and his son, Tipu Sultan, expanded the kingdom and become known for their resistance against British incursions into India. The much-loved Tipu Sultan, also known as the "Tiger of Karnataka," was killed in 1799, and the Wodeyar family claimed his throne. By the beginning of the 19th century, the British Empire reigned in Karnataka and renamed the state "Mysore." On November 1, 1973, the name was officially changed back to Karnataka.

IN THE FIELD: FISH COMMUNITIES

While a Ph.D. candidate at the Gatty Marine Laboratory at the University of St. Andrews in Fife, Scotland, Amerada Bhat undertook a study of the species diversity of fish in four rivers in the Western Ghats: Sharavati, Kali, Bedti, and Aghanashini. Each river faces different ecological challenges that affect the fish communities in different ways. Specifically, Bhat studied the diversity and composition of the fish species found in the four rivers, the distribution patterns of these species, the variation of species compositions, the correlation of fish community structure with environmental gradients, the feeding ecology of some of the species, and how human disturbances might be affecting fish communities.

For two years, Bhat collected data on the fish, on the streams where the fish lived, and on the chemical characteristics of the water and the vegetation. Collections were made at 24 sites at different times of the year, during both the day and at night. Some sites represented the natural condition of the rivers and other sites represented "human disturbances," such as pollution discharge. The sites selected were at different elevations in the mountains.

Bhat identified a total of 10,771 individual fish belonging to 92 species. Some 25 species were *endemic*, or native, to the Western Ghats. Among his findings was a new species of catfish, *Batasio sharavatiensis*. The research also revealed that the Sharavati River boasts the highest richness of species; the Aghanashini River, the lowest. The Bedti River had the highest abundance of fish. Some 28 species were found in all four rivers. Downstream regions showed a higher species richness than upstream regions, a finding due to changes in stream habitat and stream physical characteristics. In summary, Bhat's research provided a method for preliminary study for preparing conservation plans in the region.

IN THE FIELD: CONSERVATION EFFORTS

Conservationists are working on several fronts to protect the Sharavati River. Some groups are concerned about the slow destruction of the river's *catchment*, or drainage basin, and others are eager to block increased tourism in the area. In January of 2005, Sunderlal Bahuguna—a top environmentalist in India—joined an Australian environmentalist in a march from the Sharavati's source to its mouth. According to the *Hindu*, India's national newspaper, the march was held "to create awareness about the importance of watersheds, to understand the historical aspects of the river and its impact on the people living along its banks, and to study the forest and biodiversity in the region."

Several conservation institutions have banded together to form the Western Ghats Forum, an organization determined to limit "human-induced threats" to the biodiversity identified by a study conducted in 2000 titled "National Biodiversity Strategy and Action Plan: Western Ghats Ecoregion." The forum is opposed to several proposed tourism projects for the regions along the Sharavati River and has called for conservation projects instead of tourism development. Along with members of the forum, scientists and naturalists from the Center for Ecological Sciences at the Indian Institute of Science in Bangalore have expressed concern about proposed campsites on some of the 125 wooded islands that exist within the reservoir created by the Linganmakki Dam.

"The wildlife here, not habituated to humans, will perish or migrate if trekking or cycling is introduced in these regions," states a position paper prepared by the scientists at the Center. The detailed report notes that the proposed tourism projects involving Kanur, Nagara, and others would have an impact on "the most biologically rich habitats" and that slight disturbance would "hamper the ecology" of that region. "Islands are known to be ecologically sensitive and more fragile than the main land," notes the report. "They are prone to invasion by non-native species and take more time (compared to the mainland) to recover from any adverse ecological changes or catastrophes."

The forum held a conference titled "Western Ghats: Conservation and Human Welfare" in September 2003 as the first step to balance the demands of "conservation and development" for the area. A second conference was held in December 2005.

THE FUTURE OF JOG FALLS

India, the second most populous country after China, now houses one-sixth of the world's total population. More than 1 billion people are spread over some 1.2 million square miles (3.1 million km²). Resources required to meet the needs of such a large population are many.

Conservation of wild places like Jog Falls is a priority of such organizations as the Western Ghats Restoration Project and the Ashoka Trust for Research in Ecology and Environment. Both organizations are based in Karnataka, the state where Jog Falls is located, and both are aware of the delicate balance that must be achieved regarding tourism in the popular state. Hosting too many tourists takes a toll on the environment, but attracting too few adversely affects the economy. These organizations and other environmentalists concerned about the Sharavati River have brought to light some of the problems associated with Jog Falls, but knowledge about the many problems facing the area may not overcome the basic needs of the Indian people.

Cumberland Falls

North America

Known as "The Niagara of the South," "Little Niagara," and "Great Falls," by any name Cumberland Falls is the largest waterfall in the United States south of Niagara Falls and east of the Rocky Mountains. The curtain of water stretches 125 feet (38 m) wide and drops 68 feet (20 m), sending 26,929 gallons (101,937 L) of water over the edge into a boulder-strewn gorge every second. During spring flooding, the width of the waterfall more than doubles. Shown in the upper color insert on page C-8, Cumberland Falls occurs on the Cumberland River in the southeastern part of Kentucky on the coal-rich Cumberland Plateau.

Cumberland Falls is known for its *moonbow*, or lunar rainbow, a muted rainbow formed under a full moon by the mist rising from the falls. Under ideal conditions, moonbows may occur at any waterfall, though the streetlights at and around many falls in populated areas obscure the phenomenon. Located on the border of McCreary and Whitley counties in the 1,675-acre (677-ha) Cumberland Falls State Park, Cumberland Falls is in a wooded area thick with birch, wild magnolia, poplar, holly, and hickory trees, far from the lights of cities or commercial areas. Visitors who show up on the night of a full moon hoping to see a moonbow are rarely disappointed. A conventional rainbow can also be seen at the base of the waterfall almost every sunny morning.

Like all waterfalls, Cumberland Falls is on the move. The waterfall originally formed as the Cumberland River broke through softer rock, causing rapids to form as the *grade*, or slope, of the riverbed changed. Further erosion caused a vertical drop. As the water continued to flow, a rock overhang developed at the top of the waterfall as water wore away, resulting in an *undercut* of the rock behind the falls—as shown in the illustration on page 120. Fractures in the rock, as well as the pressure of the water, eventually caused the overhang to split and crash into the river below.

The process was repeated numerous times, and in this way, Cumberland Falls slowly moved upstream. Geologists say that originally the waterfall was some 45 miles (72 km) downstream from its current location. Cumberland Falls was higher at the earlier site than it is today, as the Laurel and Rockcastle Rivers added to its volume. As Cumberland Falls continues to recede, the drop will shorten, and after a long period of time, the waterfall will erode back into rapids. No rate of erosion has been calculated, and no predictions have been made on the current rate of retreat.

A second, little-known waterfall at Cumberland Falls State Park exists as a direct result of the recession of Cumberland Falls. Eagle Falls, about 1,800 feet (548 m) downstream from Cumberland Falls, occurs in a narrow ravine on Eagle Creek, dropping 44 feet (13 m) into a rock-filled channel surrounded by woods. Eagle Falls, shown in the lower color insert on page C-8, developed when Cumberland Falls retreated up the valley, leaving a *hanging valley*, or a valley that forms a cliff face above the main

© Infobase Publishing

The process of undercutting, shown here, allows a waterfall to migrate upstream.

valley because the lower part has been eroded. About 150 feet (45 m) from the base of Eagle Falls, Eagle Creek joins the Cumberland River.

THE CUMBERLAND RIVER

The 16th-largest river in the United States, the Cumberland River travels 687 miles (1,105 km) through the mountains of Kentucky and Tennessee and empties into the Ohio River at Smithland, Kentucky, some 12 miles (19 km) upstream from the mouth of the Tennessee River. The Cumberland River begins near Harlan, Kentucky, at the junction of three small streams—Poor Fork, Clover Creek, and Martin's Fork—some 120 miles (193 km) upstream from Cumberland Falls. Elevation at the source of the Cumberland River is 1,575 feet (480 m). With a population of more than half a million, Nashville, Tennessee, is the largest city along the river.

From its source to Cumberland Falls, the Cumberland River is considered a wild mountain stream that runs shallow during late summer but swells with heavy flooding during winter and spring. The river crosses the Cumberland Plateau above the falls between Williamsburg, Kentucky, and the Kentucky-Tennessee state line, flowing in a gorge between cliffs 300 to 400 feet (91 to 121 m) high. After traveling a short distance in Tennessee, the river turns north and crosses western Kentucky to the Ohio River.

The drainage area of the Cumberland River is 18,080 square miles (46,826 km²). The average flow is 24,064 gallons (91,092 L) per second. When flooding, the river has reached a maximum flow of 445,838 gallons (1,687,680 L) per second, but in times of drought, the flow has dropped as low as 29 gallons (109 L) per second. Elevation along the Cumberland River ranges from 1,800 feet (548 m) along the highest ridge to 800 feet (243 m) by the edge of the river.

Fast-moving rapids characterize the Cumberland River above Cumberland Falls. Because of the presence of locks and dams, the river is navigable below Lake Cumberland, a 50,250-acre (20,335-ha) reservoir created by the Wolf Creek Dam. The river is known for its catfish and bass, and trout live in the tributaries.

Lake Cumberland, some 10 miles (16 km) from Cumberland Falls, was built in 1950, primarily to control flooding on the river and to aid in the production of hydroelectric power through the Wolf Creek Dam. Built for about $80.4 million, Lake Cumberland boasts some 1,085 miles (1,746 km) of shoreline. A popular recreation spot with over 5 million visitors each year, Lake Cumberland holds 1.9 trillion gallons (7 trillion L) of water, or enough water to cover the entire state of Kentucky with three inches (7 cm) of water. The six turbines at the Lake Cumberland *power plant*—the building that houses equipment to convert water to

THE MAN WHO NAMED THE RIVER

Dr. Thomas Walker—a physician, pioneer, surveyor, and onetime guardian to Thomas Jefferson—named the Cumberland River in 1750 after Prince William Augustus of England, the duke of Cumberland, who sponsored Walker's expedition into the area. Beating the more storied Daniel Boone by 17 years, Walker built the first cabin in Kentucky near the river he named, and a replica of that cabin stands on the site today.

Walker was an agent for the Loyal Land Company of Virginia when he led a four-month-long expedition through the Cumberland Gap, a pass through the Cumberland Mountains region of the Appalachian Mountains near the junction where the borders of Kentucky, Tennessee, and Virginia meet. Elevation at the pass is 1,600 feet (487 m). Originally formed by an ancient creek, the gap served as the chief passageway before 1810 for some 200,000 to 300,000 immigrants journeying from the east coast over the Appalachian Mountains and into Kentucky and the Ohio Valley. Walker and his team explored the area for land suitable for settlement. His journal described "plentiful wildlife, thickly tangled woods, and rugged terrain."

Of British ancestry, Walker was born on January 25, 1715, in King and Queen County, Virginia, where his family lived as prosperous plantation owners. He attended the College of William and Mary and studied medicine under his brother-in-law, Dr. George Gilmer of Williamsburg. In 1741, Walker married Mildred Thornton Meriwether, a second cousin to George Washington. The couple had 12 children.

Walker served as physician to Peter Jefferson, Thomas Jefferson's father, and was named Thomas Jefferson's guardian after the senior Jefferson's death. All three men shared a passion for exploration. In 1743 Walker led an expedition to what now is known as Kingsport, Tennessee, and that trip cemented his reputation as a surveyor. Throughout his life, Walker worked as a surveyor and land agent as well as a doctor. He was also active in civil affairs, serving as a treaty commissioner, a member of the House of Burgesses and General Assembly, a delegate to the Revolutionary Convention, and a member of the Committee of Public Safety.

Thomas Anbury, author of *Travels through the Interior Parts of America*, wrote this about Walker: "One day, in a chat, while each was delivering his sentiments of what would be the state of America a century hence, the old man [Walker], with great fire and spirit, declared his opinion that 'The Americans would then reverence the resolution of their forefathers, and would eagerly impress an adequate idea of the sacred value of freedom in the minds of their children, that if, in any future ages they should be again called forth to revenge public injuries, to secure that freedom, they should adopt the same measures that secured it to their brave ancestors.'" Thomas Walker died on November 9, 1794.

electricity—are capable of producing enough electricity to supply the annual needs of a city with a population of 375,000.

Several other lakes and dams were also developed on the Cumberland River as part of the Tennessee Valley Authority system, an agency created by Congress in May 1933 to redevelop the area. Other large power plants and dams along the river include Dale Hollow Dam on the Obey River near Celina, Tennessee, and Center Hill Dam on Caney Fork, southeast of Carthage. Other dams include Old Hickory Dam, Cheatham Dam, and Barkley Dam.

Several Civil War battles occurred near the Cumberland River, including the battle for Fort Donelson, fought February 11–16, 1862, in Stewart County, Tennessee. Union forces took the fort, a move that opened the Cumberland River as an avenue of invasion of the South. This same battle elevated Brigadier General Ulysses S. Grant from an obscure and largely unproven leader to the rank of major general. Grant earned the nickname "Unconditional Surrender Grant" in this battle, and the Union Army of the Cumberland was named after the river.

CANYONS, ARCHES, AND CAVES

All of the Cumberland River's chief tributaries enter downstream from Cumberland Falls. The rivers include the Laurel, Rockcastle, South Fork, and Little River in Kentucky and the Obey, Caney Fork, Stones, Harpeth, and Red in Tennessee. These rivers have created the dramatic landscape of the area by cutting through rock to carve gorges and canyons, and leaving behind cliffs and ridges, natural rock arches, and waterfalls.

The 29,000-acre (11,735-ha) Red River Gorge Geological Area, about two hours from Cumberland Falls, is a canyon system in east-central Kentucky. Designated a National Natural Landmark in 1976, the Red River Gorge was formed some 300 million years ago. The canyons present an intricate maze of narrow, winding ridges and valleys separated by steep slopes and continuous bands of high *sandstone* cliffs. Sandstone is a clastic sedimentary rock, or a rock made up of fragments of other rocks. In 2003, the National Park Service named 37,000 acres (14,973 ha) in and around the Red River Gorge a National Archaeological District, and listed it on the National Register of Historic Places.

More than 100 natural rock arches occur in the Red River Gorge Geological Area, the greatest concentration of arches in the United States east of the Rocky Mountains. The largest of the sandstone and limestone formations is Sky Bridge, a 90-foot (27-m) span of solid rock, shown in the photograph on page 124. Moonshiner's Arch, also known as Sandgap Arch, is 10 to 12 feet (3 to 3.6 m) high and 36 feet (10 m) wide with a span of 42 feet (12 m).

Some 6,000 to 8,000 caves are found along the limestone cliffs of the Daniel Boone National Forest, which shares boundaries with Cumberland Falls State Park. The caves are home to many aquatic species and bat populations, some of them rare and some of them dependent on specific environmental conditions for breeding and hibernation. Because the air inside a cave is stable and most often dry, caves provide a protective environment for fossils and prehistoric artifacts. Caves also draw the interest of hikers and *spelunkers*, people who explore caves.

Sky Bridge is one of more than 100 sandstone and limestone formations in the Red River Gorge Geological Area in Kentucky. *(www.kentuckytourism.com)*

THE CUMBERLAND PLATEAU

Cumberland Falls lies on the western edge of eastern Kentucky in a region known as the Cumberland Plateau, a flat-topped tableland that rises over 1,000 feet (304 m) above the rest of the region and extends from Pennsylvania to Alabama. About 285 million years ago, the region gradually began to lift due to the collision between the continental plate and the neighboring oceanic plate. Over thousands of years, erosion on the Cumberland Plateau has sculpted sheer cliffs, steep-walled gorges, rock shelters, waterfalls, and natural rock bridges and arches.

The Cumberland Plateau—also known as the Appalachian Plateau— boasts rocky terrain, a moderate climate, and a good deal of rain. The soil is thin and infertile, though at one time a dense hardwood forest grew here, similar to those in the Appalachian Mountains, which lie just 60 miles (96 km) to the east. Hopes for the future of forests in the area were boosted in 2005 when a giant paper company that is the largest landowner on the Cumberland Plateau agreed to stop clear-cutting natural hardwood forests.

The Eastern Kentucky Coal Field, which covers 10,500 square miles (27,194 km²) and contains about 52 billion tons (47 billion metric tons) of remaining resources, sits on the eastern edge of the Cumberland Plateau, which is called the Pottsville or Cumberland Escarpment. The escarpment is *stepped*, or tiered, due to alternating layers of hard sandstone and less resistant *shale*, soft, fine-grained sedimentary rock made of consolidated mud and clay.

The rocks that now make up the top layer of the Cumberland Plateau were laid down in an ancient shallow sea during the Mississippian Period (360 to 320 million years ago) and the Pennsylvanian Period (320 to 296 million years ago). The rocks were deposited in horizontal layers thousands of feet thick, and the weight of these layers atop one another hardened the sediments into layers of sandstone, shale, *limestone*—sedimentary rock that contains the remains of innumerable shells of microscopic and macroscopic sea creatures—and *coal*, a dark sedimentary rock that contains a high percentage of organic plant material.

The Cumberland Plateau is the source of much of the coal mined in Kentucky and Tennessee. Coal, like petroleum and natural gas, is a *fossil fuel*, or a natural product derived from a previous geologic time that is used for fuel. Coal contains carbon, hydrogen, oxygen, nitrogen, and sulfur, with smaller amounts of other materials such as aluminum and zirconium. Coal had its beginning as plants that grew in swamps hundreds of millions of years ago. The shifting of the Earth over vast spans of time compressed and altered the plant remains to produce four different grades of coal: lignite, sub-bituminous, bituminous, and anthracite.

Coal is produced in 22 states today. In recent years, Wyoming has been the nation's top coal-producing state, providing 373.2 million short tons (338 metric tons), or about 30 percent of the national total. West Virginia ranks second and Kentucky third. The three states accounted for 58 percent of total U.S. coal production. Even as coal production declines, coal consumption is on the rise as the nation seeks alternatives to oil.

EARLY SETTLEMENTS

Though Native Americans living on the Cumberland Plateau certainly knew of Cumberland Falls, explorer Zachary Green is credited with discovering the waterfall during an expedition in 1770. He named the falls for its river.

Six different cultures have been identified as residing in Kentucky from 13,000 B.C.E. to 1650 C.E.: the Paleo-Indian Culture; the Archaic Culture; the Woodland Culture; the Adena Culture; the Mississippian Culture, and the Fort Ancient Culture. From 1650 until 1750, Shawnee tribes from north of the Ohio River and the Cherokee and Chickasaw tribes from south of the Cumberland River fought for control of the land they called "The Great Meadow," but no Indian nation held possession of the land. The ruling Chickamaugans called the Cumberland River *Ta-Eache*, which translates as "River of the Blue Flute." The southern river Shawnee tribe called the waterway "the River of the Shawandasse."

In 1750 and 1751, Dr. Thomas Walker led the first expeditions into Kentucky. After the outbreak of the French and Indian War in 1754, all exploration in the region ended for at least a decade. In 1767, famed explorer and frontiersman Daniel Boone visited Kentucky. He returned two years later for further exploration. The first permanent settlement in Kentucky was built in 1774 at the site of present-day Harrodsburg. Boonesboro was established in 1775, and other settlements followed soon after.

In 1776, Kentucky was named a county of Virginia, but soon after the end of the American Revolution, Kentuckians began to rally for separation. In 1792, after nine conventions to discuss the details, Kentucky was declared a separate state and was admitted to the Union as the 15th state. Frankfort was chosen as the state capital. In 1818, state officials purchased what is now the westernmost region of Kentucky from the Chickasaw tribe and annexed the land.

Though Kentucky was officially neutral in the Civil War, the state supplied approximately 100,000 troops to the North and 40,000 troops to the South. The Union president, Abraham Lincoln, and the Confederate president, Jefferson Davis, were born one year apart in Kentucky in log cabins within 100 miles (160 km) of each other. After the Civil War, Kentucky turned to tobacco farming and production. Coal mining, which began on a large scale in the 1870s, was well established in Kentucky by the early 20th century. The mines boomed during World War I, but after the war, the demand for coal lessened and production declined.

IN THE FIELD: MUSSEL MAN

Just as the deaths of canaries in coal mines once served as the early warning system to notify miners of dangerous air pollution and lack of oxygen, the health of freshwater mussels is an indicator of water quality in rivers, streams, and lakes. Mussels require clean water to survive, so changes in the life span or behavior of mussels indicate that water quality is suffering. Poor water quality, of course, may be hazardous for other species in the area, including humans.

James B. Layzer, Ph.D., has studied mussels since 1988, some of them in Kentucky rivers. Layzer is a research scientist with the U.S. Geological Survey and is currently stationed at Tennessee Tech University's Center for the Management, Utilization and Protection of Water Resources. One of his recent studies looked at the reproduction of the mussel *Megalonaias nervosa* in the Cumberland River. Scientists had reason to believe that water temperature had changed, thereby possibly affecting the mussels' rate of reproduction.

Layzer and his colleague Jackie H. Oven collected mussels from the Cumberland River and moved them to the Tennessee River. They held other mussels in a bay at Kentucky Lake. One year later, samples of the same species of mussel were taken from the Cumberland River, Kentucky Lake, and the group that had been relocated to the Tennessee River.

Layzer found that relocated mussels and mussels originating in Kentucky Lake had undergone normal reproductive development, but there was no indication of reproductive activity in individuals collected from the Cumberland River. These results indicate that the altered temperature regime is disrupting the normal cycle.

Layzer's report also noted that the reproductive cycle of other endangered species of mussels in the Cumberland River had most likely been disrupted as well. The Wolf Creek Dam and another nearby dam are the causes of what Layzer called "unnaturally cold water." Dams release water from the bottom of the reservoirs, and that water is quite cold. The colder water does not affect the trout just below the dams—or the trout fishermen who gather there—but Layzer notes that the mussel populations will eventually die out due to lack of reproduction.

STEWARDSHIP OF THE FALLS

Cumberland Falls and the land surrounding it were held privately from the 1860s to the 1930s. T. Coleman DuPont, a Kentucky native and a U.S. senator from Delaware, frequently visited the area. When he learned in 1930 of plans to build a dam at the site, DuPont purchased 600 acres (242 ha) surrounding the falls and donated it to the state of Kentucky. He urged officials to establish a state park on the land.

DuPont died later that year, but state officials fulfilled his wishes. They bought additional land adjacent to the donated land, and in 1933 the state legislature set aside the area as Kentucky's third state park. A lodge bearing DuPont's name was erected in the early 1930s. The original burned in April 1940, but the lodge was rebuilt and opened in 1941. The lodge houses accommodations for visitors as well as a museum that features Native American artifacts and exhibits relating to area plants, animals, and history.

Cumberland Falls State Park occupies state-owned land within the Daniel Boone National Forest, a wooded treasure that encompasses more than 704,000 acres (884,898 ha) of rugged terrain with over 600 miles (965 km) of trails. Rivers and streams course through the forest, and rocky cliffs provide additional habitat for plants and animals.

One species that prefers moist, cool, shaded crevices in a north-facing cliff is the uncommon filmy fern. In contrast, the white-haired goldenrod, a threatened species, prefers drier nitrate-rich soils found at the base of cliffs. The endangered Virginia big-eared bat is one of the rare animals in the Daniel Boone National Forest. The bat, which is a mammal, hibernates in winter and raises its young in the spring in the many dark caves found in the woods. Green salamanders, which use their sticky toes to climb up and down steep rock, are another species found along cliffs in the forest.

In addition to the state park that surrounds it and proximity to a national forest, Cumberland Falls is the centerpiece of a 1,290-acre (522-ha) nature preserve. Dedicated in September 1983, Cumberland Falls State Park Nature Preserve exists to protect Cumberland Falls, the Cumberland River, and several species of rare plants and animals. Some of the protected plants include Lucy Braun's white snakeroot, brook saxifrage, star tickseed, Rand's goldenrod, and spiked hoary-pea. Rare animals include the green salamander, several insects—the caddis fly among them—and three endangered mussels. With three official safeguards in place, the Niagara of the South appears to be protected from any and all encroachments, except for the natural geological changes that inevitably alter every waterfall—and every other landform—on Earth.

Glossary

❖❖❖❖❖❖❖❖❖❖✦❖❖❖❖❖❖❖❖❖❖

aa   a type of lava flow that leaves a rough, fragmented surface

aluminum oxide   an abrasive made primarily of bauxite

anthracite   coal that is almost pure carbon

archipelago   a group of islands

basalt   the most common form of lava

batholith   an immense mass of igneous intrusive rock that comprises the core of many mountain ranges

bauxite   a material containing aluminum hydroxide minerals, silica, iron oxide, titanium, and aluminosilicate

caldera   a collapsed volcanic crater

cap rock   a layer of hard rock that overlays softer rock at the top of a waterfall

carnivorous plant   a plant that eats insects

catchment   a drainage basin

cavitation   the phenomenon where small cavities form in fluid, then rapidly collapse, sending out shock waves and potentially disintegrating nearby rock

cirque   a steep-sided, hollow amphitheater

clastic   composed of fragments of older rocks, such as sandstone

coal   a dark sedimentary rock that contains a high percentage of organic plant material

differential erosion   erosion that occurs at varying rates, caused by the differences in the resistance of surface materials

discharge   a volume of water moving through any one place at one time

dolostone   a type of limestone originally formed on the bed of an ancient sea that has hardened with the addition of several minerals

endemic   native; "indigenous" is a synonym

escarpment   a vertical cliff at the edge of a plateau or ridge

exfoliation   a weathering process, mainly caused by freeze-thaw cycles, causing granite to weather in large, thin sheets

extrusive igneous rock   a rock that was vented at the surface as volcanic lava and then cooled and crystallized at the surface

faults   rock fractures where land has been significantly displaced

fossil fuel   a natural product derived from a previous geologic time that is used for fuel

gap   a breach in a mountain

geode   a hollow, spherical rock with crystals lining the interior wall

ghat   a Hindi word for mountain pass or mountain range

glacial rebound   the phenomenon where the earth rises after thick layers of ice melt

glacier   a river of ice

gneiss   a metamorphic rock similar to granite that contains banding, or alternating layers, of minerals

grade   the slope of a streambed

gristmill   a mill for grinding grain

hanging valley   a valley that forms a cliff face above the main valley because the lower part has eroded away

hot spot   an ongoing flow of magma deep in the ocean

hydrologist   a scientist who studies surface water and groundwater

hypabyssal rocks   small masses of rock that occur in strips or sheets

ice boom   a floating chain of pontoons and steel cable strung across a river to keep ice from clogging the water

ice bridge   a mound of ice that stretches across a river above the water

indigenous   native; the term *endemic* is a synonym

intrusive igneous rock   a rock that forms when magma, or molten rock, cools and hardens underground

iron ore   a mineral from which metallic iron can be extracted for use in the production of steel

joint   a surface of parting or fracture in a rock, without displacement

kupuna   an elder in the Hawaiian Islands

leprosy   a chronic, infectious disease that affects the nerves, skin, and eyes

lignite   the lowest grade of coal

limestone   a sedimentary rock that contains mainly calcite, some clay, and shells of sea creatures

mafic lava   dark-colored lava

magma   molten lava

mesa   a flat-topped mountain

mobile belts   the edges of continents where tectonic activity, such as earthquake and volcanic zones, remain active

monsoon   a wind pattern that results in heavy rain

moonbow   a lunar rainbow that occurs on some waterfalls on the night of a full moon

mountain torrent   another term for waterfall; used in the Pyrenees Mountains

pahoehoe   a type of lava flow that has a curved, smooth surface

pass   a geological feature lower than the surrounding mountains

Pele   the mythical goddess of volcanoes

plate tectonics   a theory that explains movement of plates, or layers, under the Earth's crust that creates changes in the surface of the land

plutonic rock   a rock formed at a considerable depth by crystallization of magma; it makes up massive rock formations in many mountainous areas

power plant   a massive building or group of buildings that houses the equipment used to produce electricity from water

quartz   a hard mineral typically found in sandstone, quartzite, or granite

quartzite cave   a cave made up of metamorphic rock formed from sandstone that has transformed into quartz

river capture   when one stream erodes in such a way that it cuts off another stream, diminishing the flow of the captured stream when the "pirate" stream rises above the point of capture

rock flour   finely ground rock derived from the grinding movement of a glacier

sandstone   a sedimentary rock formed from the eroded material of igneous, metamorphic, and other rocks that consolidate under the heat and pressure of burial

seamount   an active underwater volcano

sediment   solid fragmental material transported and deposited by water, ice, or wind that forms in layers in loose, unconsolidated form

schist   a soft metamorphic rock that is often green in color

shale   a soft, fine-grained sedimentary rock made of consolidated mud and clay

shield   an ancient, geologically stable zone typically found in the central section of a continent

silica   the white or colorless crystalline compound of silicone dioxide, which is the composition of the most common mineral group in the world

sima   a large shaft in a cave caused by erosion and collapses on the surface

sinkhole   a depression in rock caused by dissolution or undermining that indicates the presence of caves below

soluble rock   a rock that can be dissolved and carried away by water, e.g., limestone, dolostone, gypsum

speleology   the study of caves

spelunker   a person who explores caves

spillway a deep channel that forms when lava pushes up through a weakened chasm

standing wave a wave that remains in a constant position because water is continually moving in the opposite direction of the wave; also known as a stationary wave

stepped tiered

strait channel

succession the process of a lake drying up, plants taking hold, meadows developing, and forests growing

talus rock debris from boulders that have crashed down from above a waterfall or steep slope; also known as scree

tepui the Pemon word for mountain

tilted fault block a landmass that has lifted into place as a result of movement beneath the Earth's crust

undercut a type of erosion where water flowing down removes softer layers of rock directly under the cap rock of a waterfall

uplift a gradual rising of the land caused by tectonic movement under the Earth's crust

vesicle a gas bubble preserved in crystallized magma

volcanic plug the core of an ancient mountain; also known as a volcanic neck

white noise a calming, unobtrusive sound at a constant pitch and intensity; also known as white sound

Books

Alt, David D., and Donald W. Hyndeman. *Roadside Geology of Oregon*. Missoula, Mont.: Mountain Press Publishing Company, 1978. Detailed explanations of specific landforms throughout the state.

Batt, Richard J. *Geological History of the Niagara Gorge*. Buffalo, N.Y.: Buffalo Geological Society, 2002. Concise synthesis of a long story.

Casteret, Norbert. *The Darkness under the Earth*. New York: Henry Holt, 1954. Exciting account of Casteret's experiences in ice caves.

Crawford, Mark J. *Physical Geology*. Lincoln, Neb.: Cliff's Notes, 1998. Quick refresher course in basic geology.

Dixon, Dougal. *The Practical Geologist*. New York: Fireside, 1992. Solid introduction to the science of the Earth.

Donnelly, Andrew. *Waterfalls*. Chanhassen, Minn.: The Child's World, 1999. Charming children's book full of color photos.

Ellwood, Brooks B. *Geology and America's National Park Areas*. Upper Saddle River, N.J.: Prentice Hall, 1996. Insightful descriptions of how the gorgeous scenery in national parks came to be.

Frank, Susan, and Phil Frank. *The Yosemite Handbook*. San Francisco: Pomegranite, 1998. Tips for visitors to Yosemite National Park, including historical information.

Gromosiak, Paul. *Niagara Falls Q&A*. 9th ed. Buffalo: Western New York Wares, 2002. Deftly answers questions both practical and quirky, many of them related to science.

———. *Seeing Niagara*. Buffalo: Western New York Wares, 2005. Provides background on history and geology, as well as information on current attractions.

Jones, William R. *Domes, Cliffs and Waterfalls: A Brief Geology of Yosemite Valley*. El Portal, Calif.: Yosemite Association, 1990. Vivid presentation of the story behind all that granite.

Kepler, Angela Kay, and Cameron B. Kepler. *Majestic Molokai: A Nature Lover's Guide*. Honolulu: Mutual Publishing, 1991. Describes the natural beauty of the island.

Lambert, David, and the Diagram Group. *The Field Guide to Geology, Updated Edition.* New York: Checkmark Books, 1998. Excellent introductory reference book, with more than 500 illustrations.

Manske, Ken. *A Traveler's Guide to the Historical Columbia River Highway.* Gresham, Ore.: M&A Tour Books, 2003. Provides opportunities for learning along the drive.

McGrain, Preston. *Geology of the Cumberland Falls State Park Area.* Lexington: University of Kentucky Press, 1966. Good overview of the landforms in the area.

Mueller, Marge, and Ted Mueller. *Fire, Faults, and Floods: A Road & Trail Guide Exploring the Origins of the Columbia River Basin.* Moscow: University of Idaho Press, 1977. Thoughtful analysis of geologic landforms written in a conversational tone.

Plumb, Gregory A. *A Waterfall Lover's Guide to the Pacific Northwest.* 4th ed. Seattle: Mountaineers Books, 2005. Information on more than 500 waterfalls in Oregon, Washington, and Idaho.

Pough, Frederick H. *Rocks and Minerals.* Boston: Houghton Mifflin, 1991. Pocketsize Peterson First Guide, perfect for beginning naturalists and rockhounds.

Stearns, Harold T. *Geology of the State of Hawaii.* Palo Alto, Calif.: Pacific Books, 1966. Excellent reference on the formation of the islands.

Sullivan, Richard. *Driving and Discovering Hawaii: Maui and Molokai.* Los Angeles: Montgomery Ewing Publishers, 2003. Mile-by-mile introduction to the island.

Sutherland, Audrey. *Paddling My Own Canoe.* Honolulu: University of Hawaii Press, 1978. Compelling account of one woman's repeated solo journeys around the wild northern coast of Molokai.

Svarney, Patricia Barnes, and Thomas E. Svarney. *The Handy Geology Answer Book.* Detroit: Visible Ink, 2004. Excellent "sound-bite" approach to geology, with plenty of solid science presented as fun facts.

Tiplin, A. H. *Geology of Our Romantic Niagara.* Ontario: Niagara Falls Heritage Foundation, 1988. Highly detailed material presented in a conversational tone.

Magazines and Newspapers

Audubon
700 Broadway
New York, NY 10003
http://www.magazine.audubon.org
Explores various environmental issues

Discover
114 Fifth Avenue
New York, NY 10011
http://www.discover.com
An excellent monthly science magazine for the general public

National Geographic
1145 17th Street NW
Washington, DC 20036-4688
http://nationalgeographic.com/ngm
Covers visible geologic features in the United States

New Scientist
6277 Sea Harbor Drive
Orlando, FL 32887
http://www.newscientist.com
Covers the latest top research news in all fields of science

Science Times in *The New York Times* (Tuesdays)
229 West 43rd Street
New York, NY 10036
http://www.nytimes.com/pages/science
Covers the latest top research news in all fields of science

Science News
1719 N Street NW
Washington, DC 20036
http://www.sciencenews.org
Covers the latest top research news in all fields of science

Web Sites

Brazil Tourism
http://www.fozdoIguaçu.pr.gov.br/turismo/ing
Official government Web site for Iguaçu Falls in Brazil

Canaima National Park
http://www.thelostworld.org/canaimanp/canaima.htm
Official Web site for the home of Angel Falls in Venezuela

Columbia River Gorge National Scenic Area
http://www.fs.fed.us/r6/columbia/forest
Official U.S. Forest Service Web site for the home of Multnomah Falls in
    the Columbia River Gorge in Oregon

Conservation International Website
http://www.biodiversityhotspots.org/xp/Hotspots
Information about threatened places and animals throughout the world

Google Scholar
http://www.scholar.google.com
This resource from Google provides access to the most up-to-date, serious
    research findings on the subjects sought.

Hawaii Volcano Tour
http://www.volcanolive.com/hawaii.html
News and plenty of photographs of Kilauea on the island of Hawaii, one of
    the most active volcanoes in the world

IncredibleIndia.org
http://www.tourismofindia.com/sts/stkarcascading.htm
Official Web site for the Indian state of Karnataka, home of Jog Falls

Kalaupapa National Historical Park
http://www.nps.gov/kala/home.htm
Official Web site for information on the peninsula on Molokai that served as
 a leper colony

Molokai: The Most Hawaiian Island
http://visitmolokai.com
Web site recommended by Molokai Tourist Commission for information on
 the island, which is the home of Kahiwa Falls.

Niagara Falls Canada
http://www.city.niagarafalls.on.ca
Official Web site for the Canadian side of Niagara Falls

Niagara Falls State Park
http://www.niagarafallsstatepark.com
Official Web site for the U.S. side of Niagara Falls

Pic du Midi Observatory
http://www.picdumidi.com/html/n1.php?content=histoire&lang=en
Official Web site of scientific observatory in the Pyrenees Mountains not far
 from Gavarnie Falls

Pyrenees National Park
http://www.parc-pyrenees.com/index_english.htm
Official Web site of Pyrenees National Park in the Pyrenees Mountains,
 home of Gavarnie Falls

World Waterfall Database
http://www.world-waterfalls.com
Excellent overview of the waterfalls of the world plus insightful articles by
 two longtime aficionados of the landform

Yosemite National Park
http://www.nps.gov/yose
Official National Park Service Web site for Yosemite National Park, home of
 Yosemite Falls

Zambia Tourism
http://www.zambiatourism.com/travel/places/victoria.htm
One of the better Web sites about Victoria Falls

Index